Candy Having Fun as Marilyn Monroe

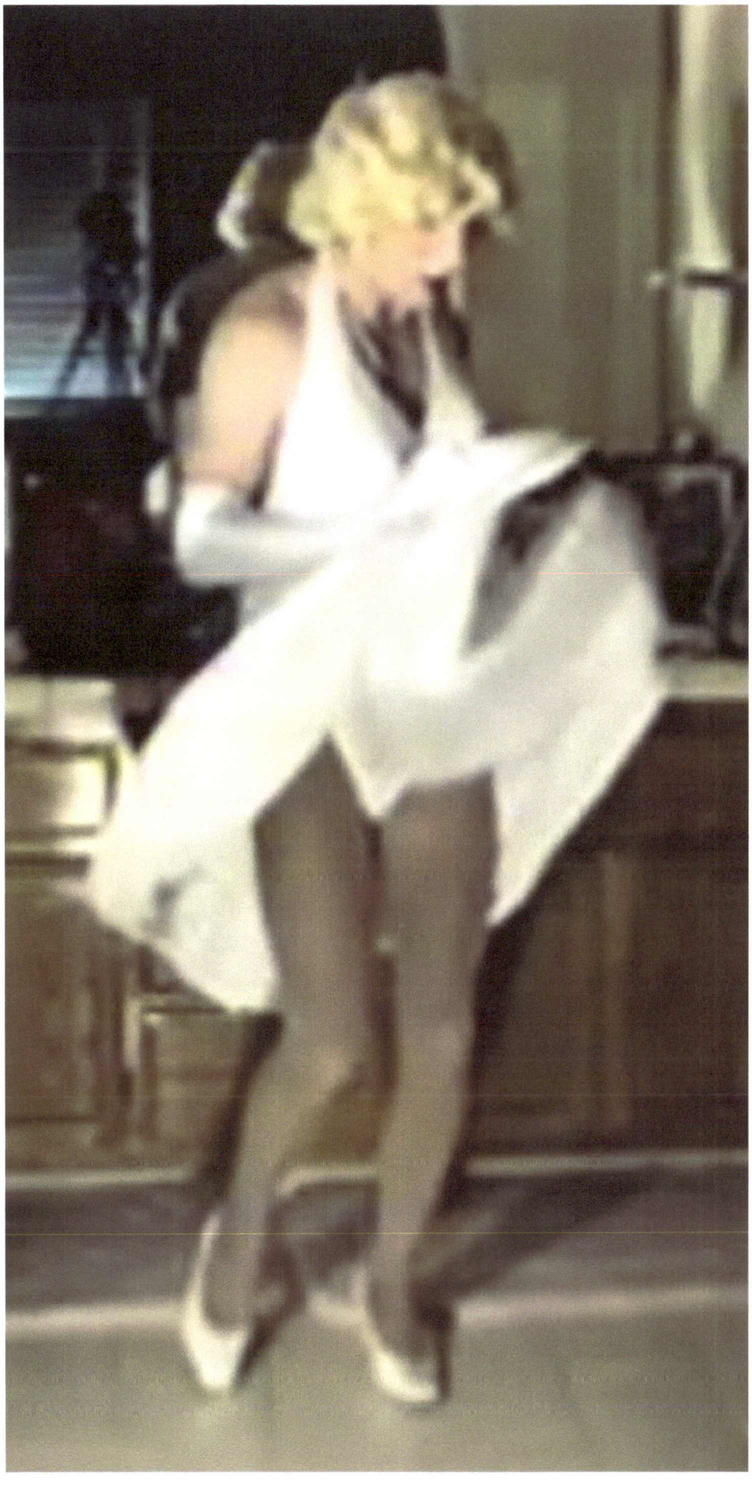

Transvestite Candy

Candy Stavroulakis

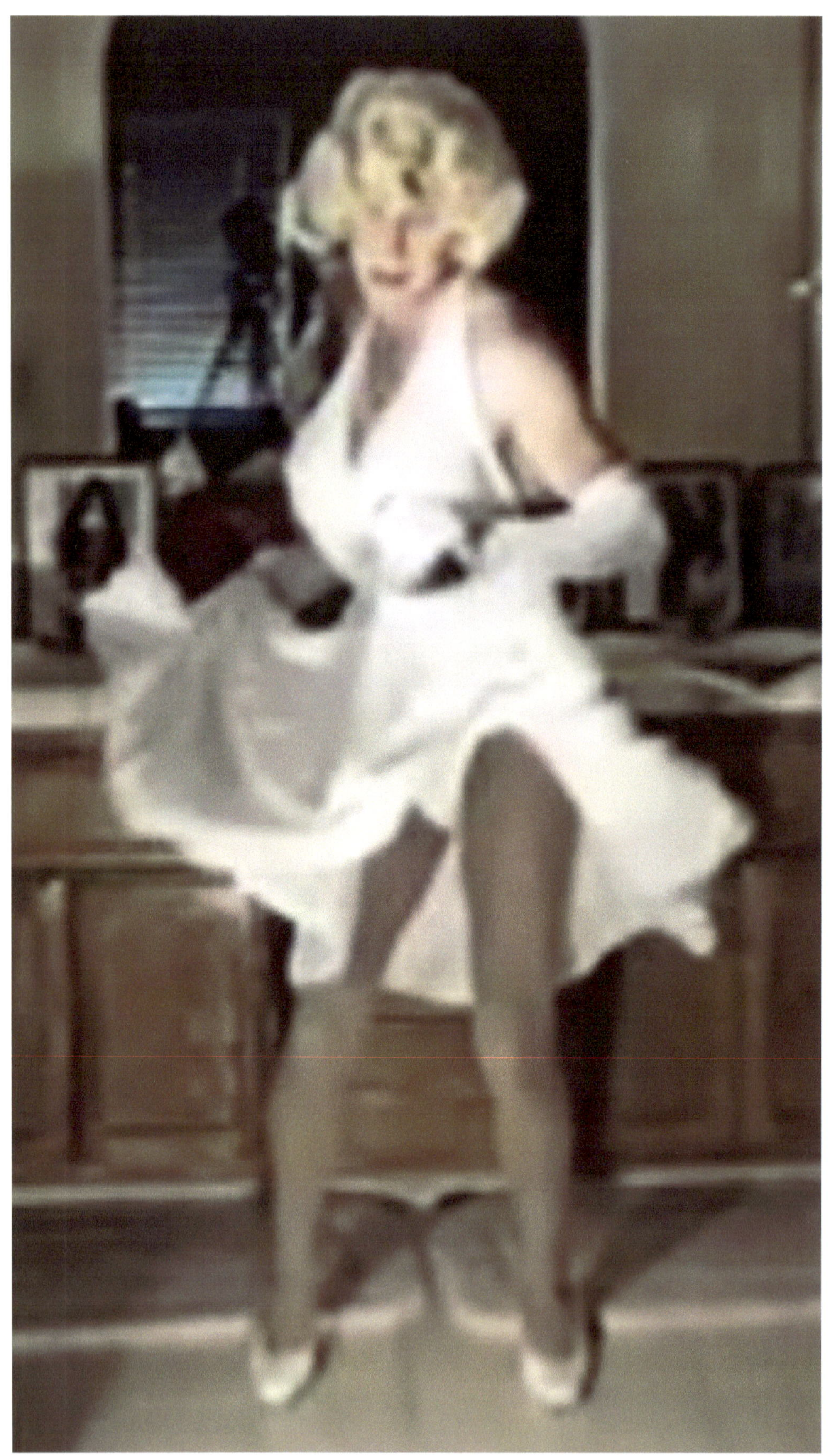

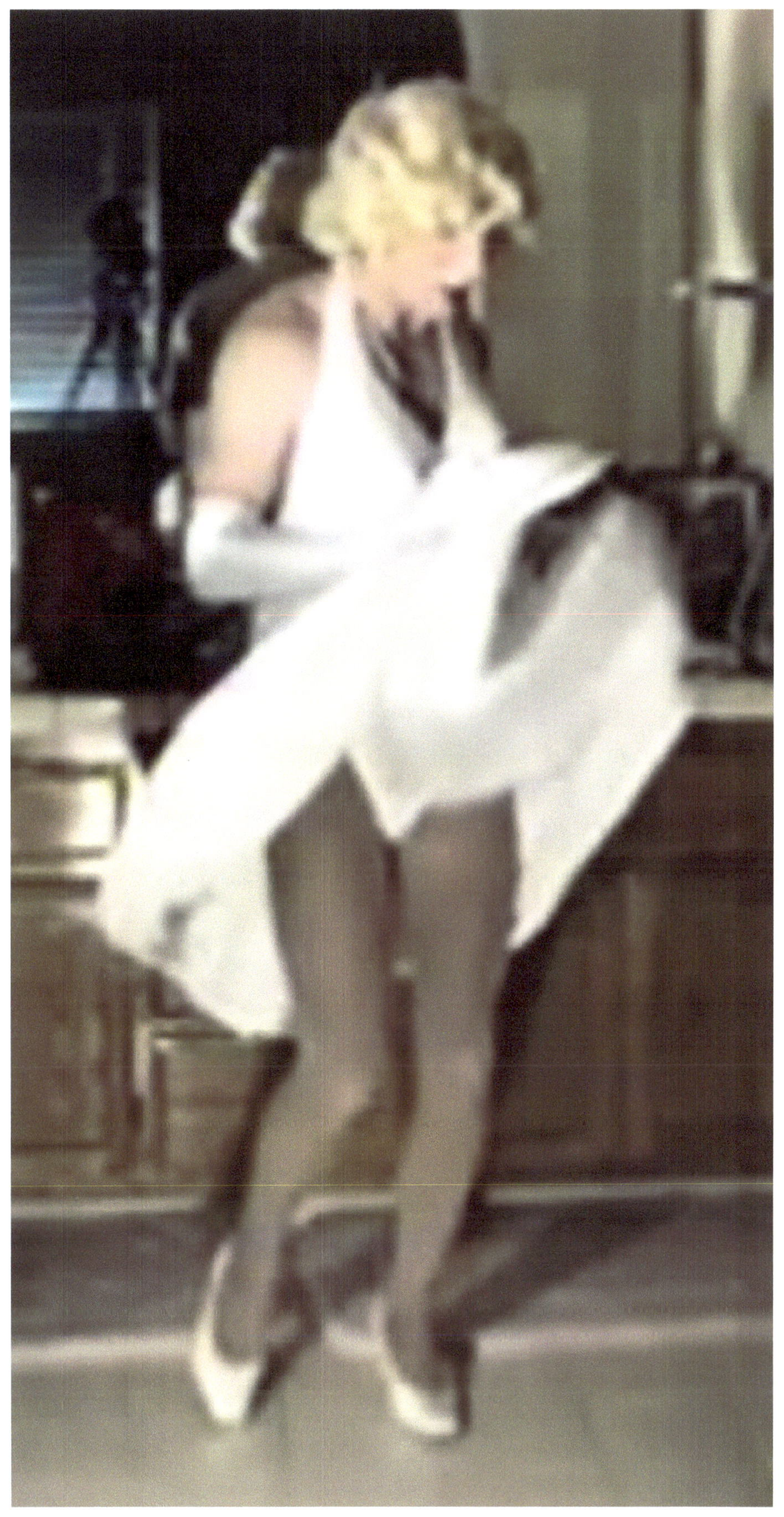

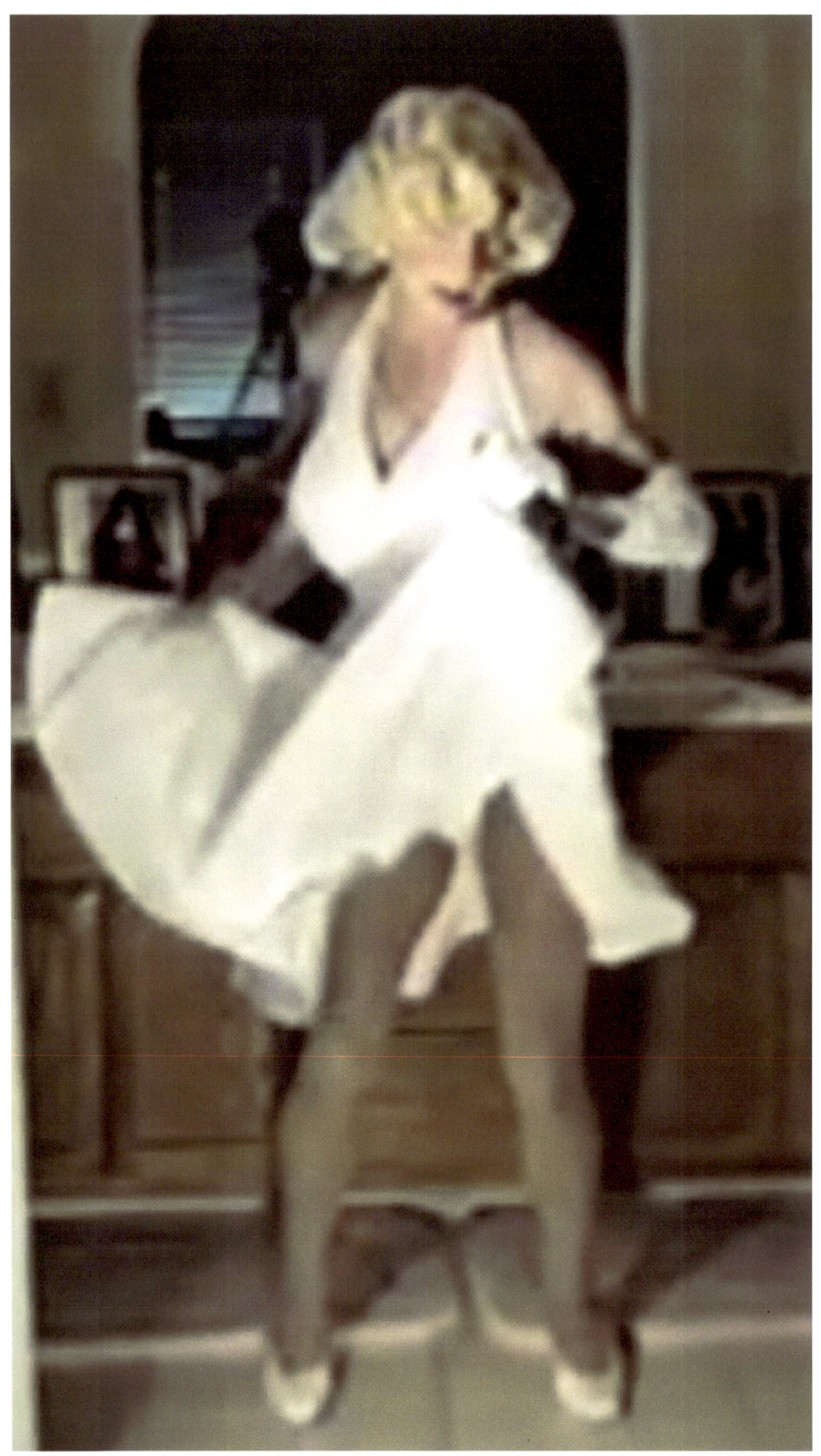

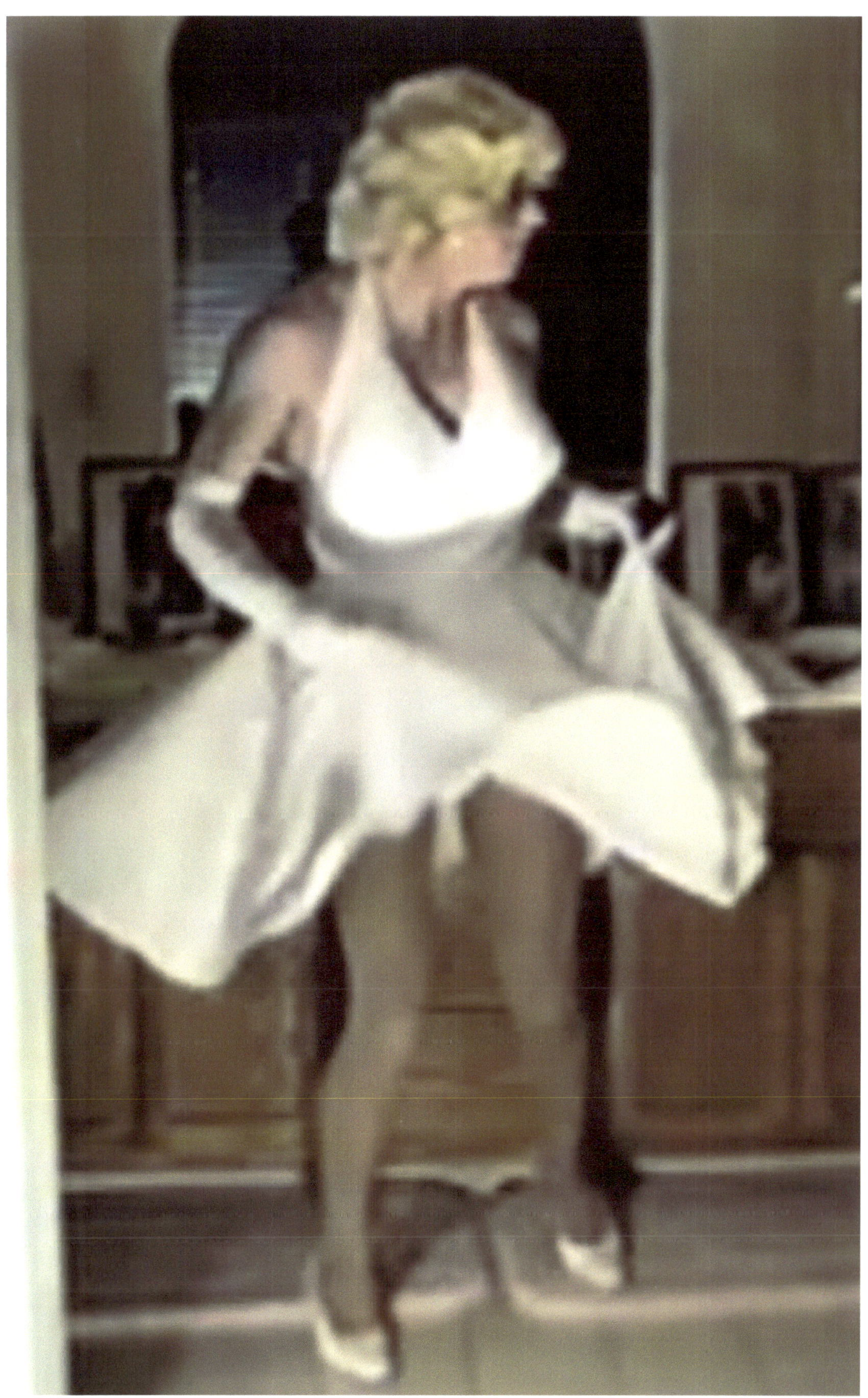

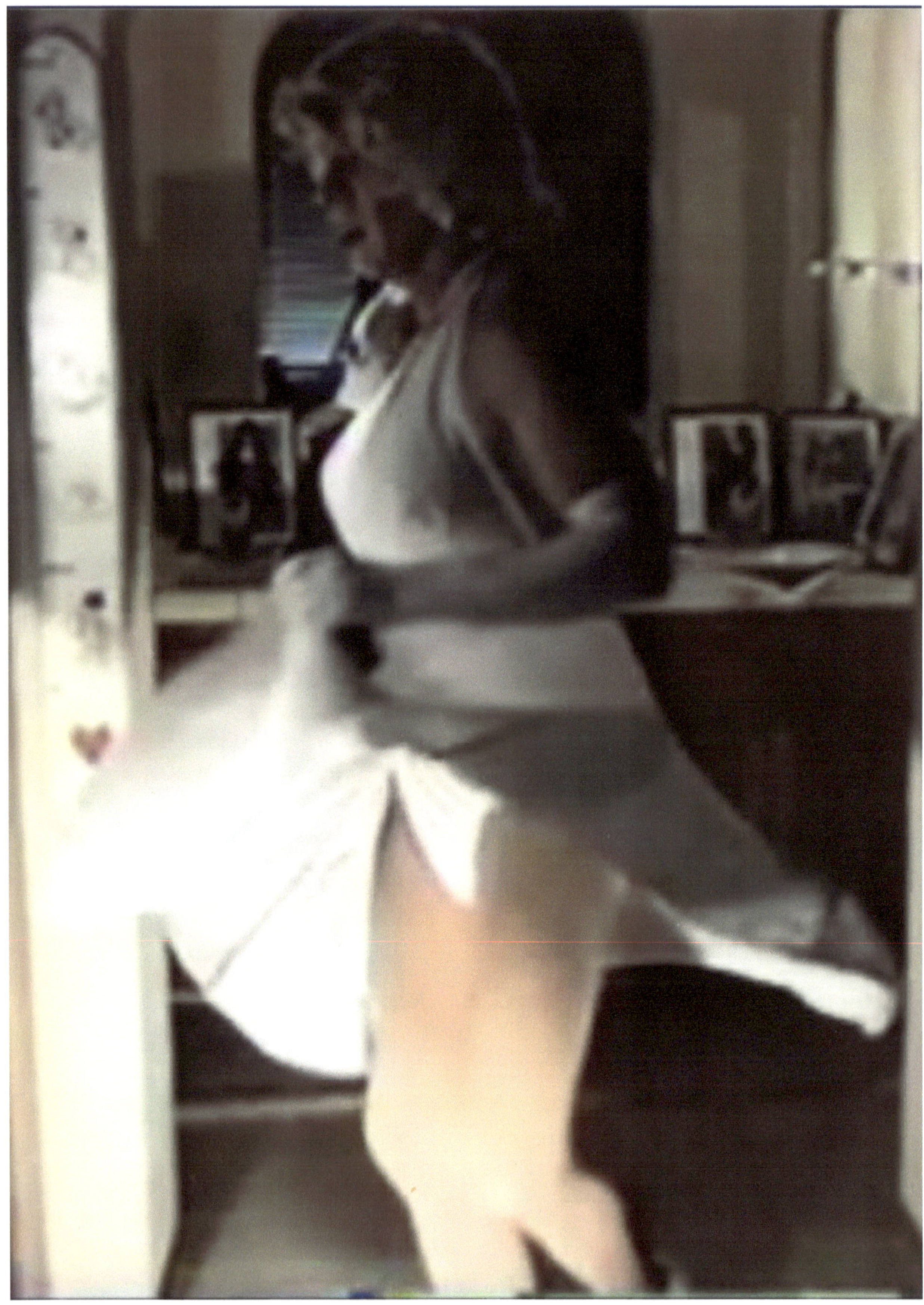

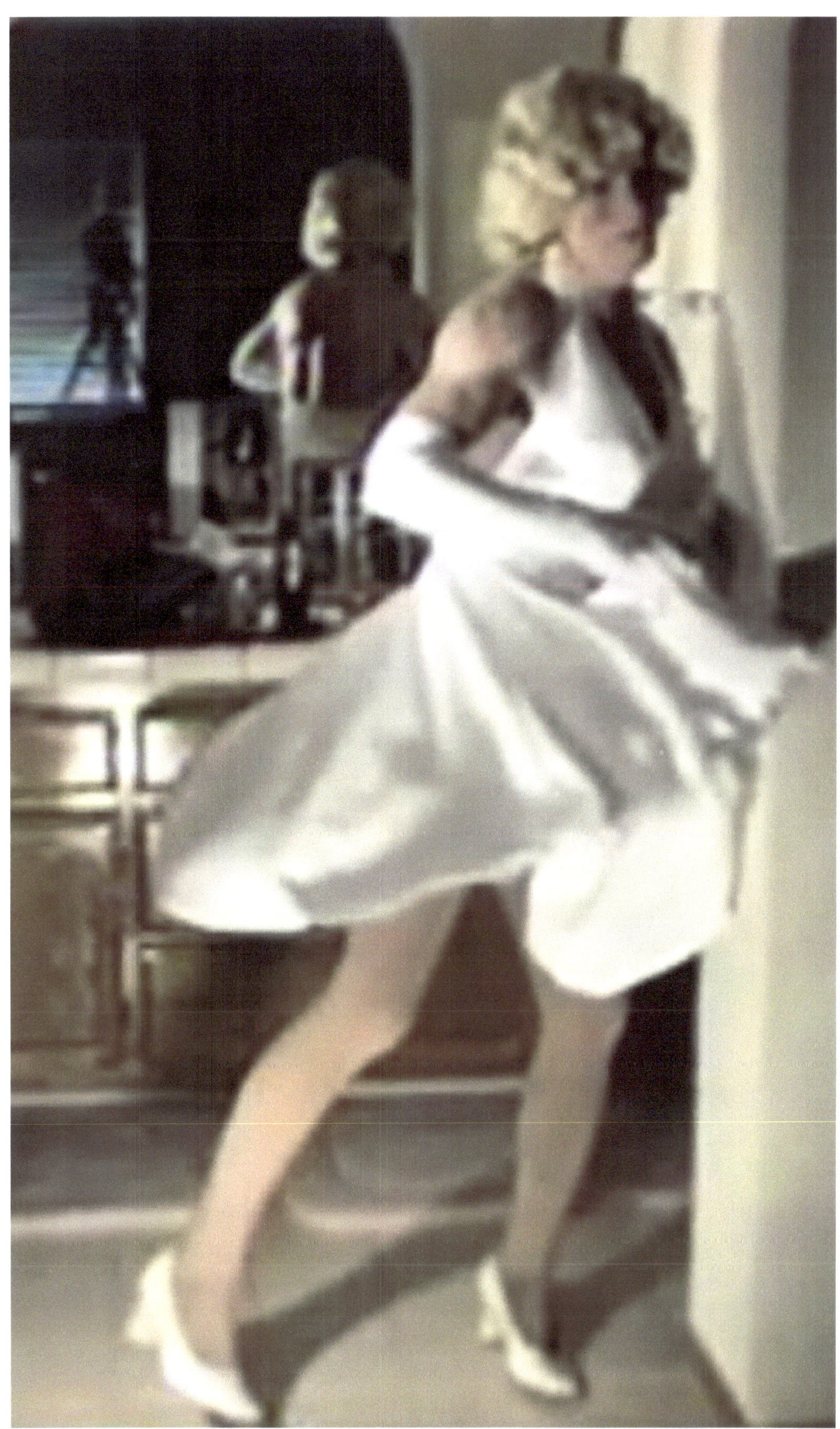

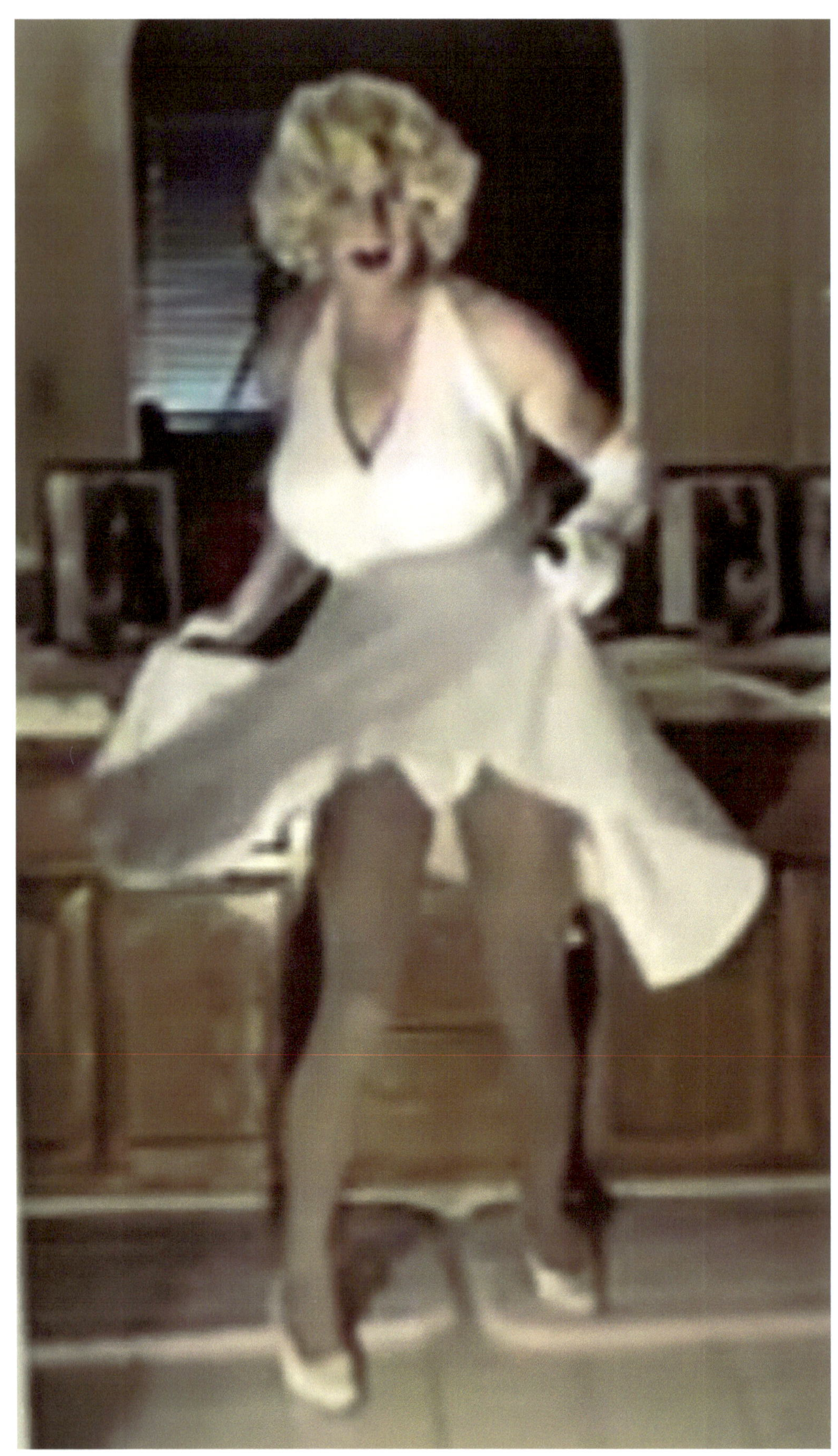

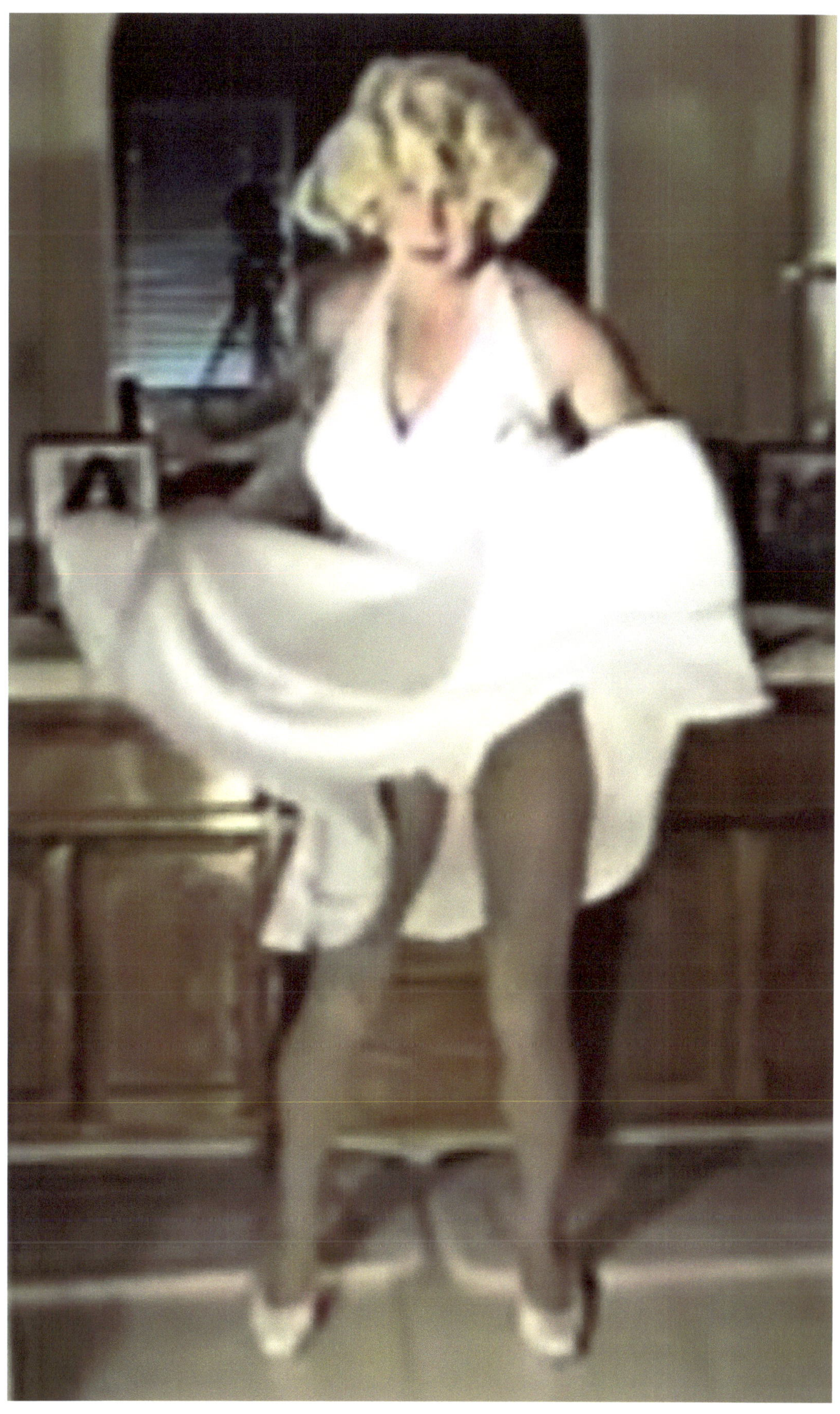

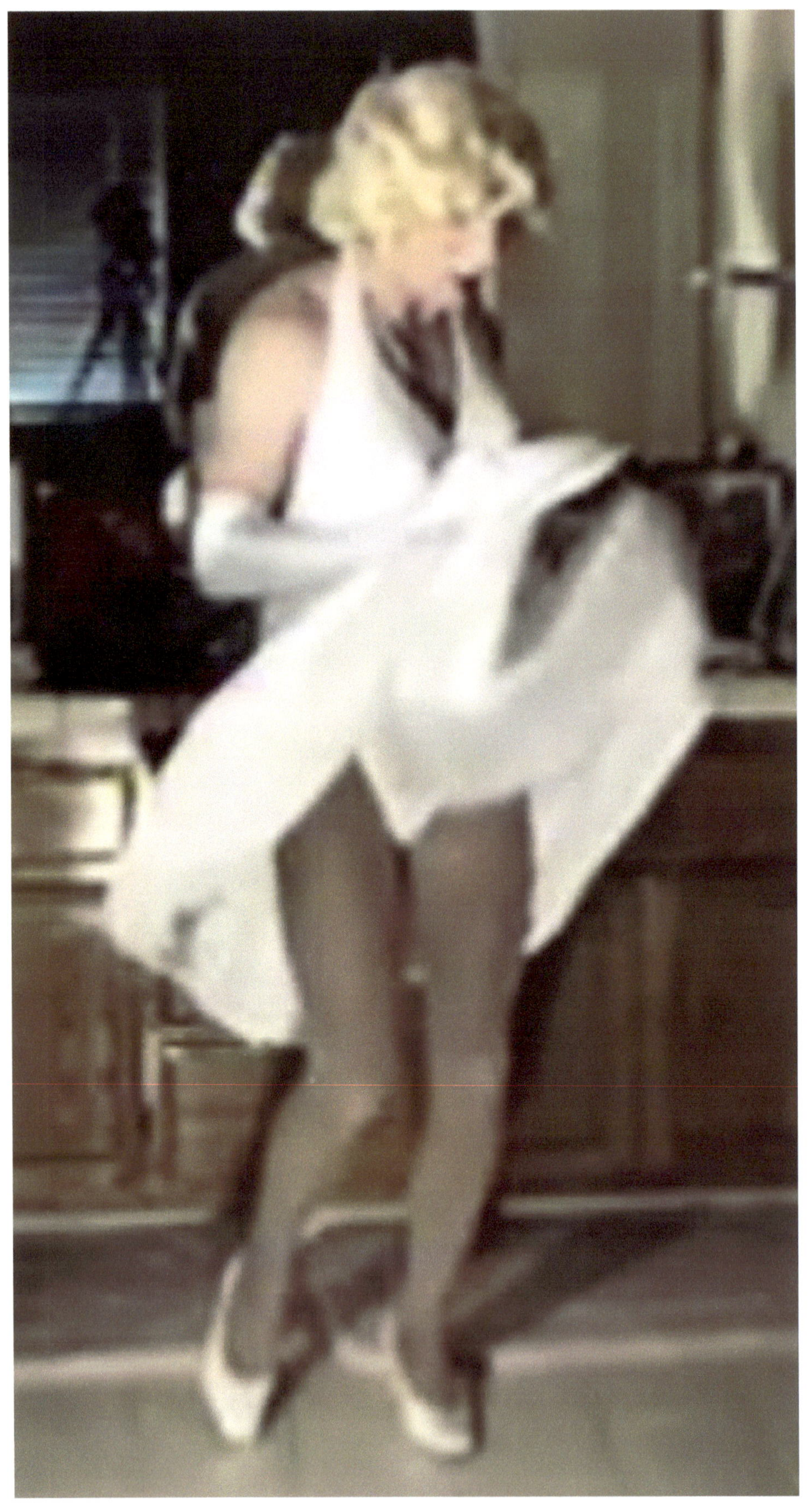

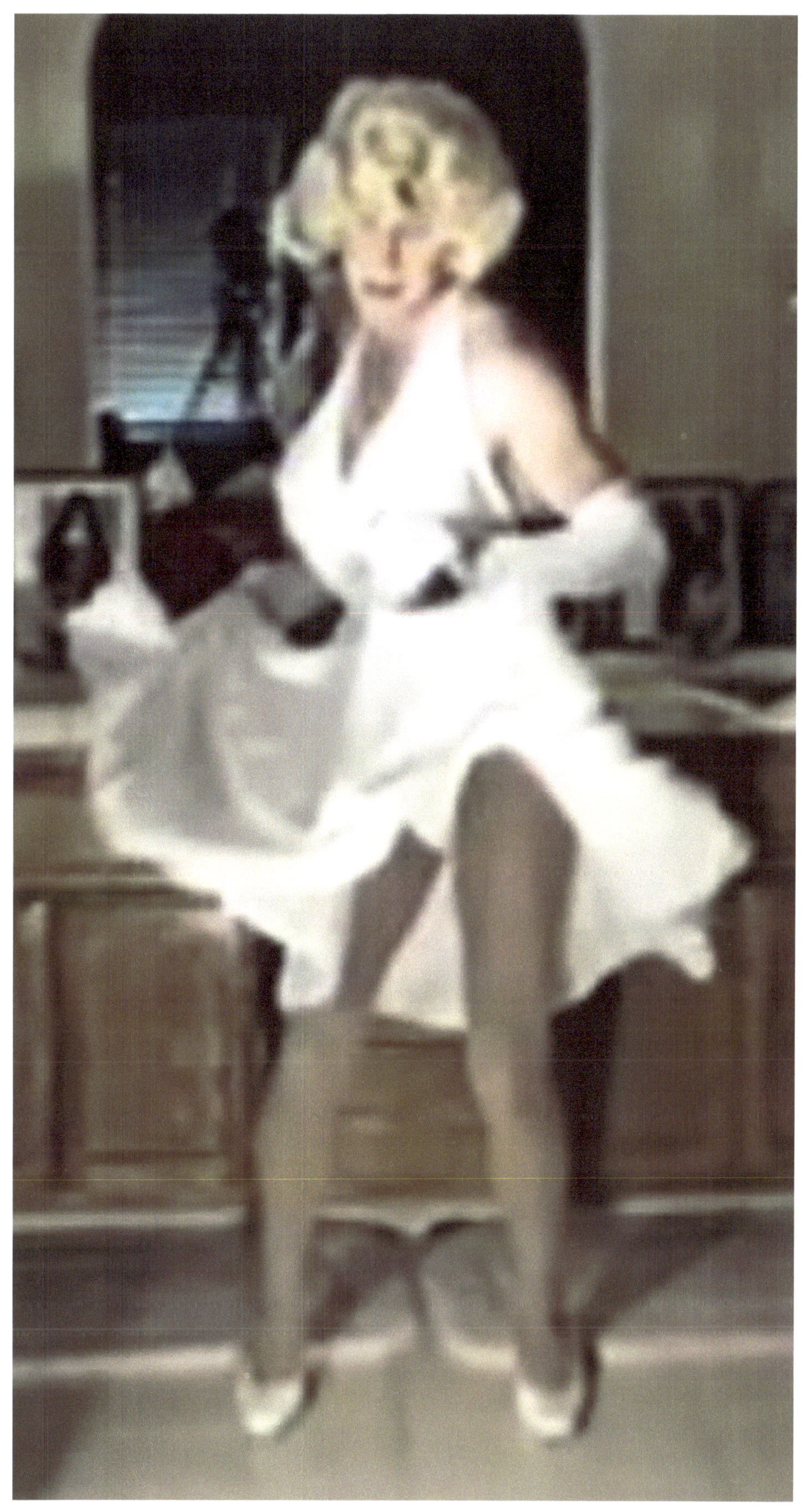

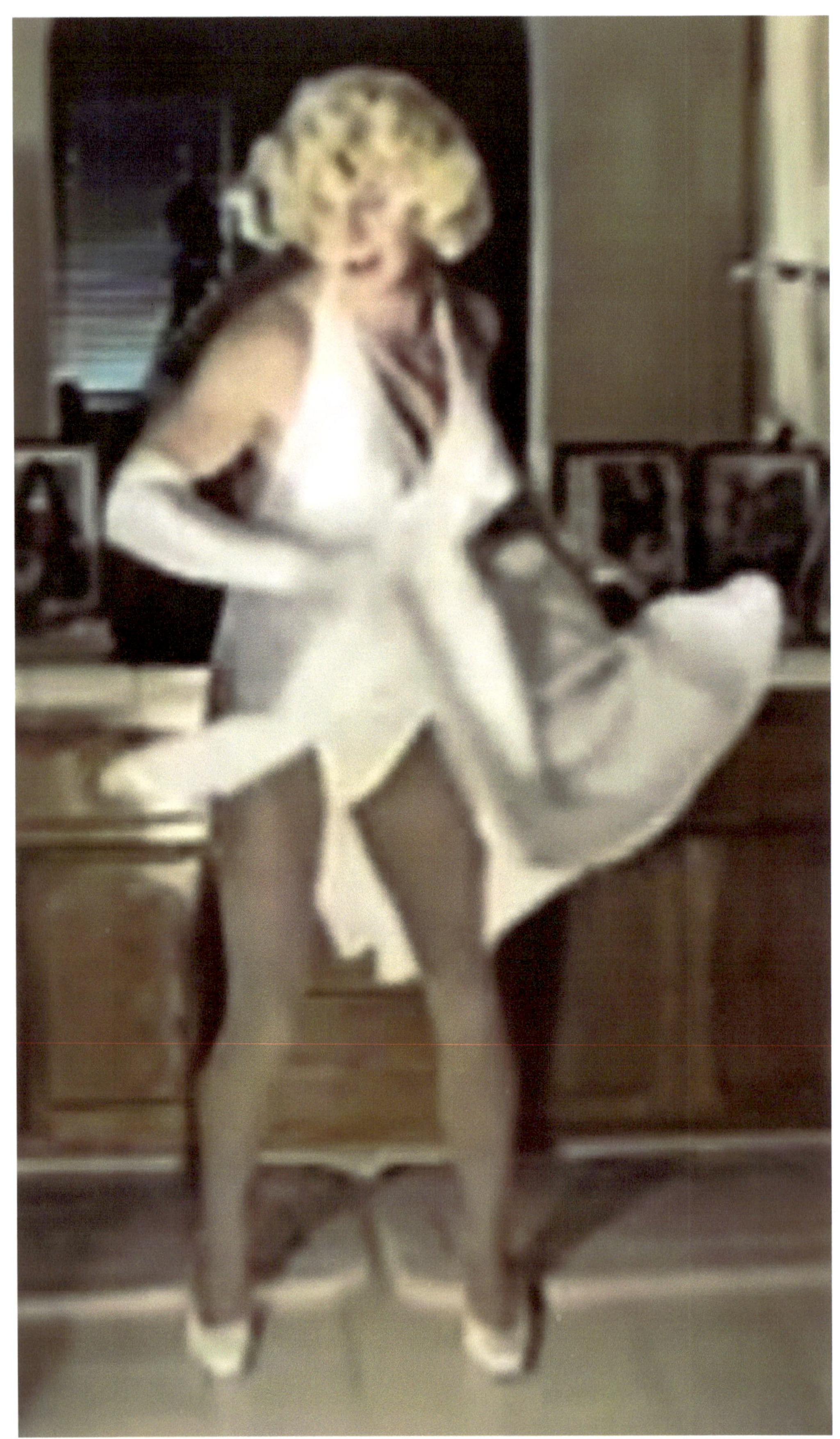

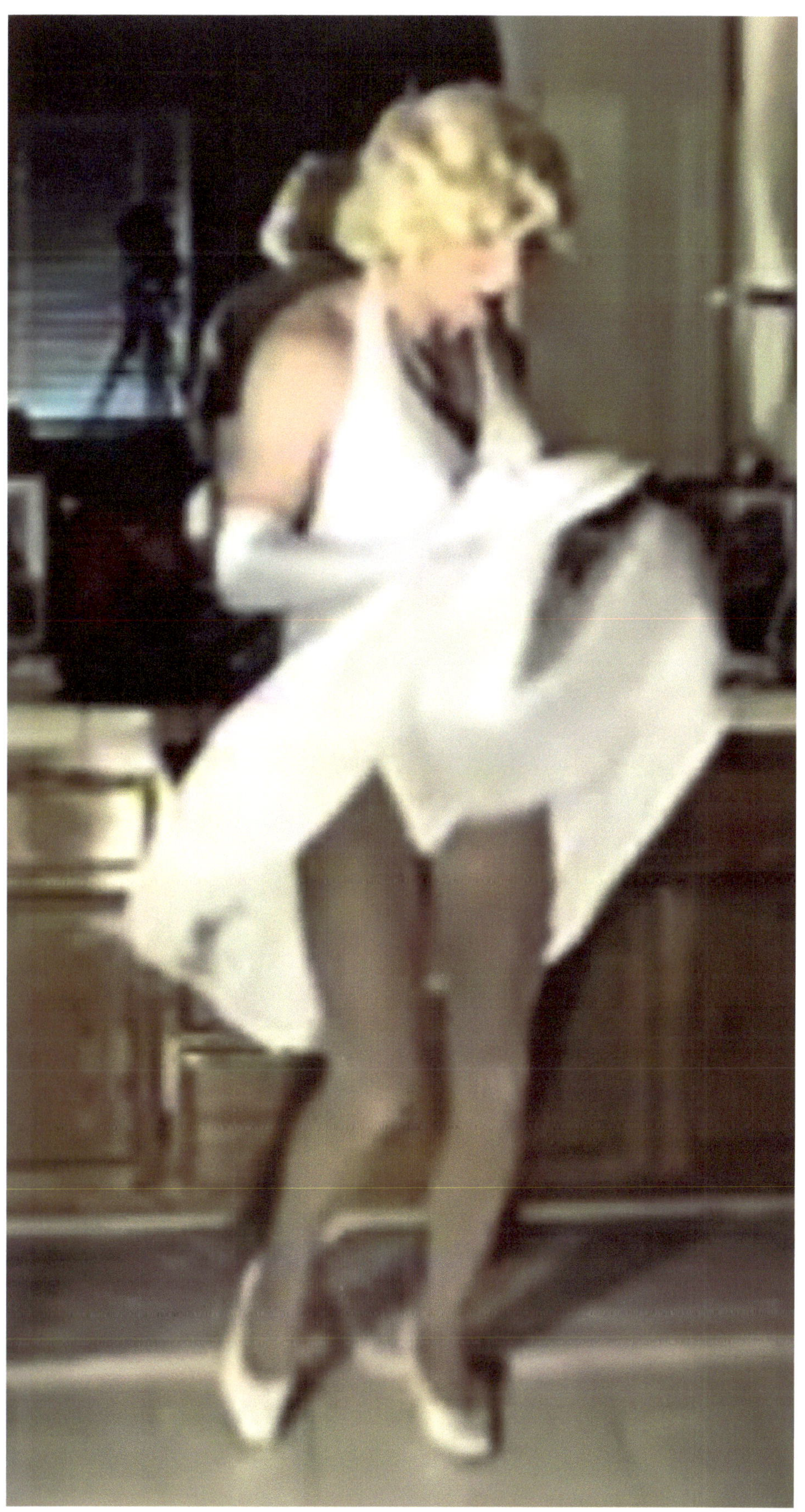

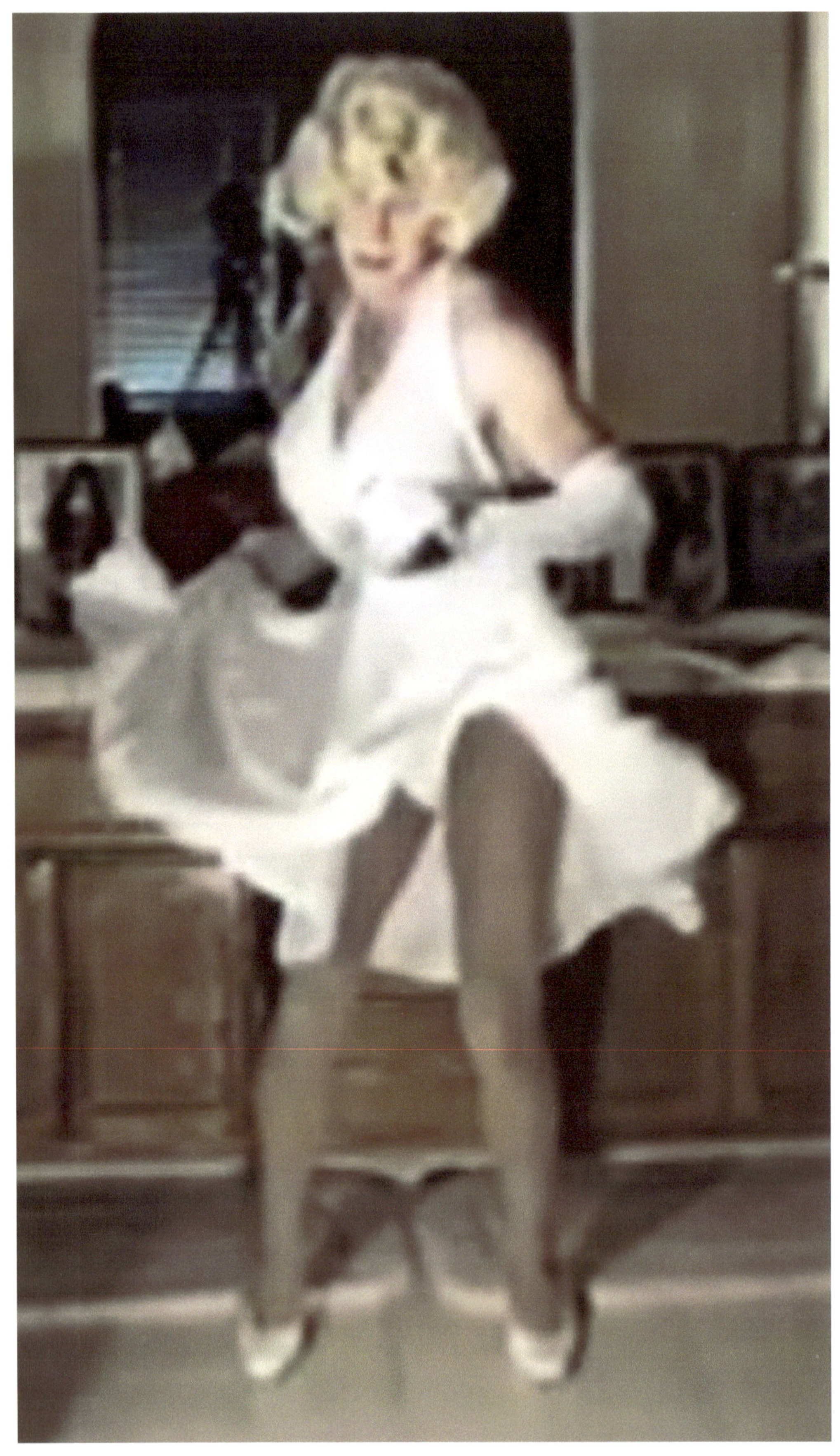

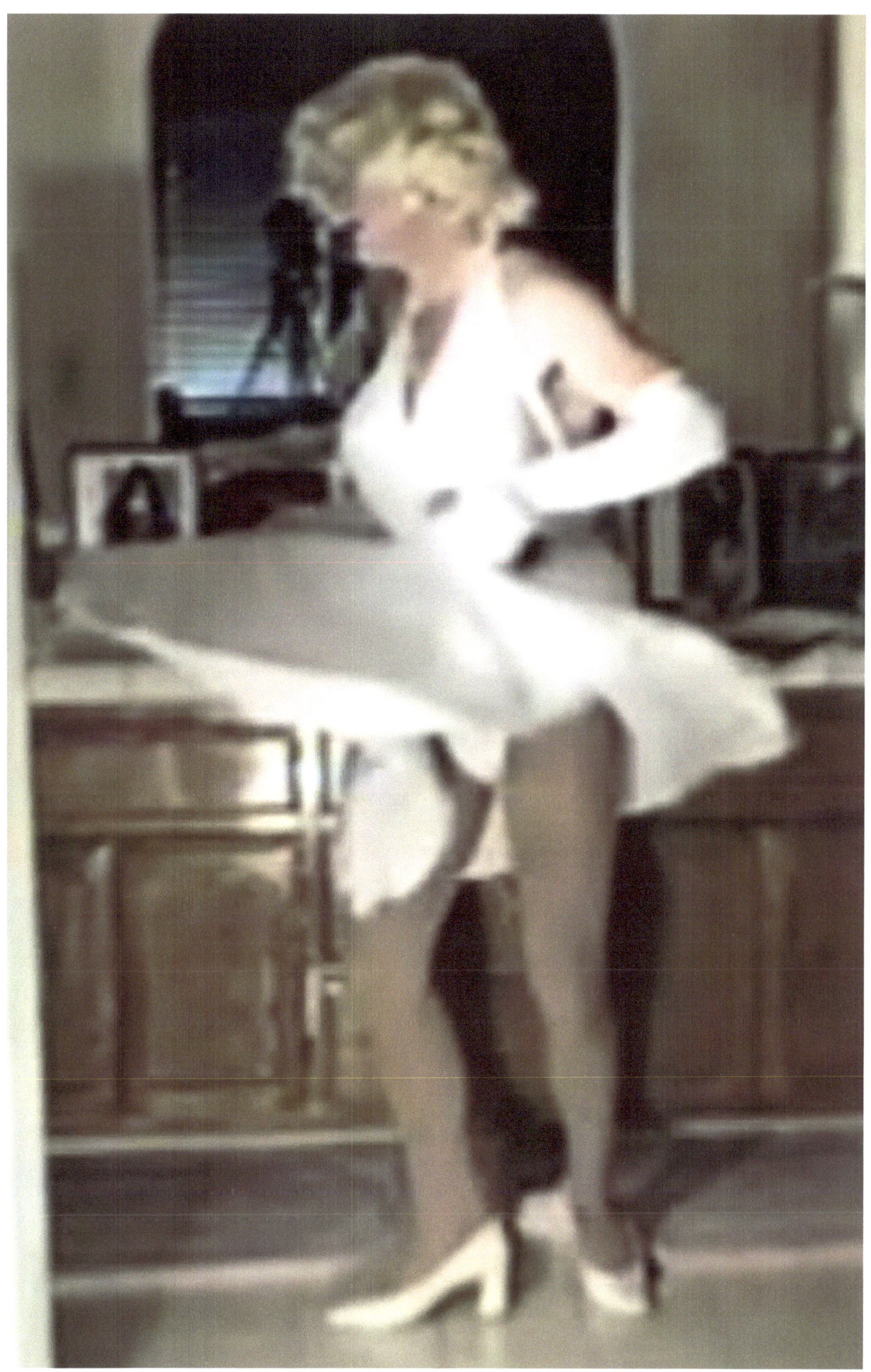

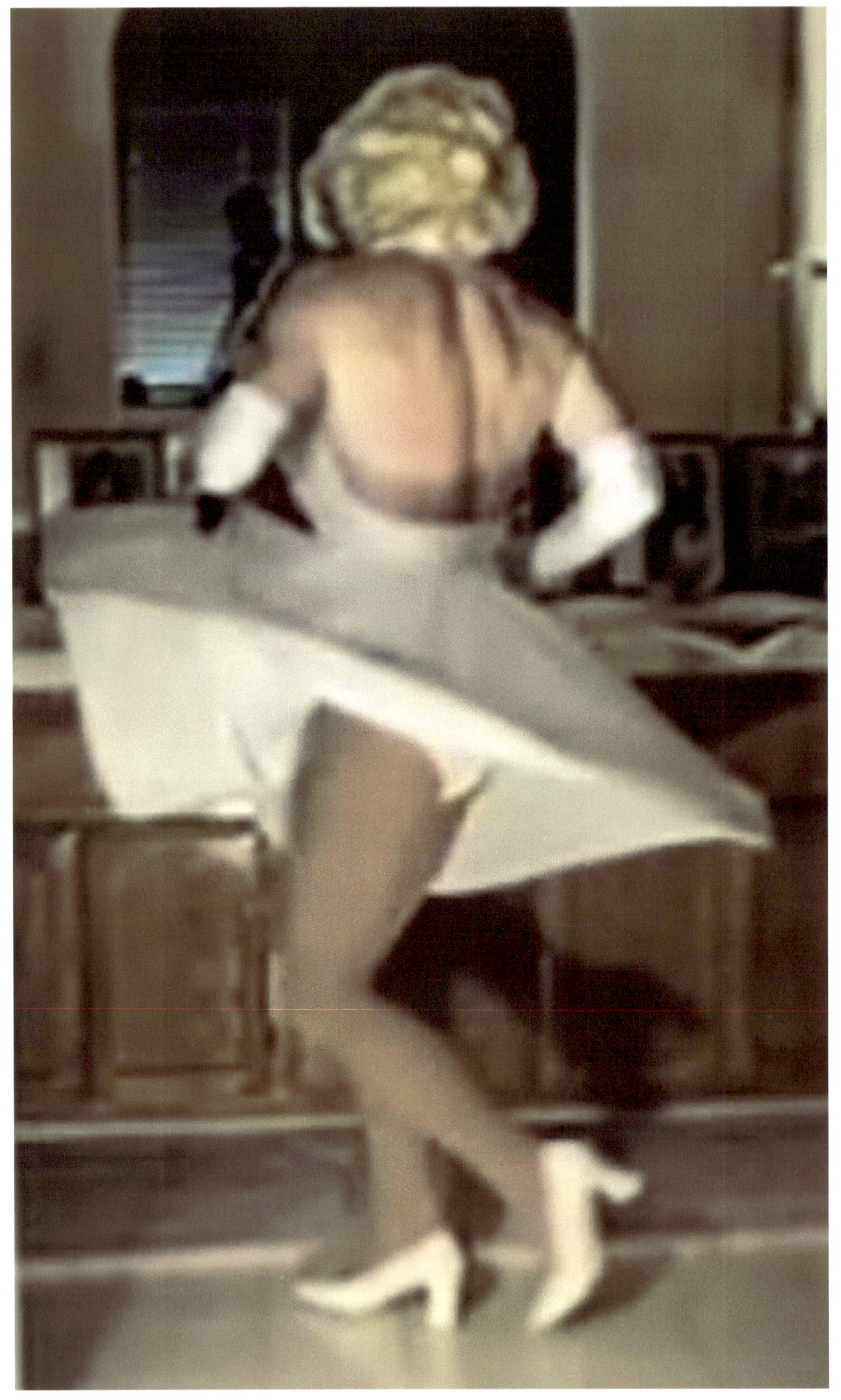

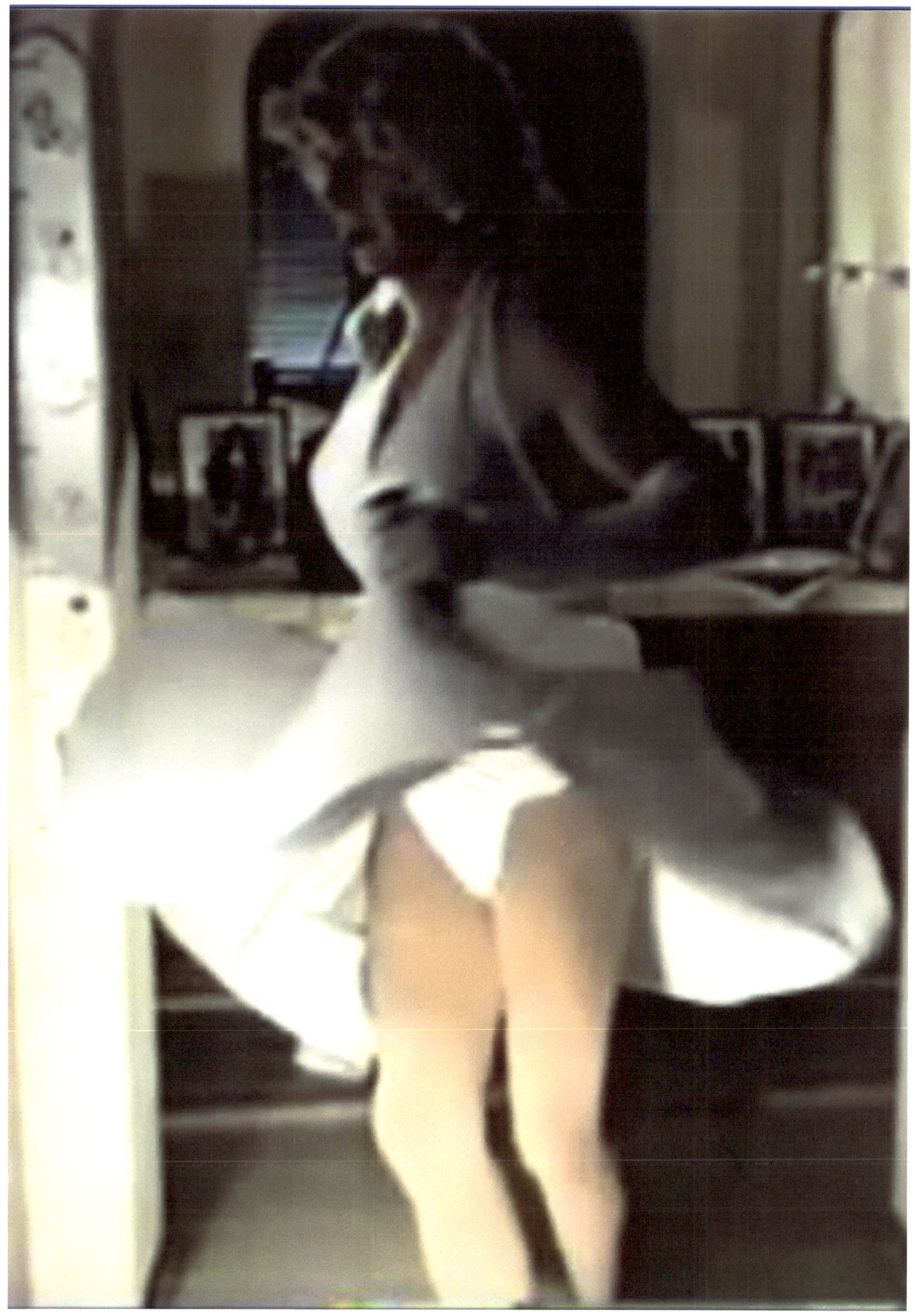

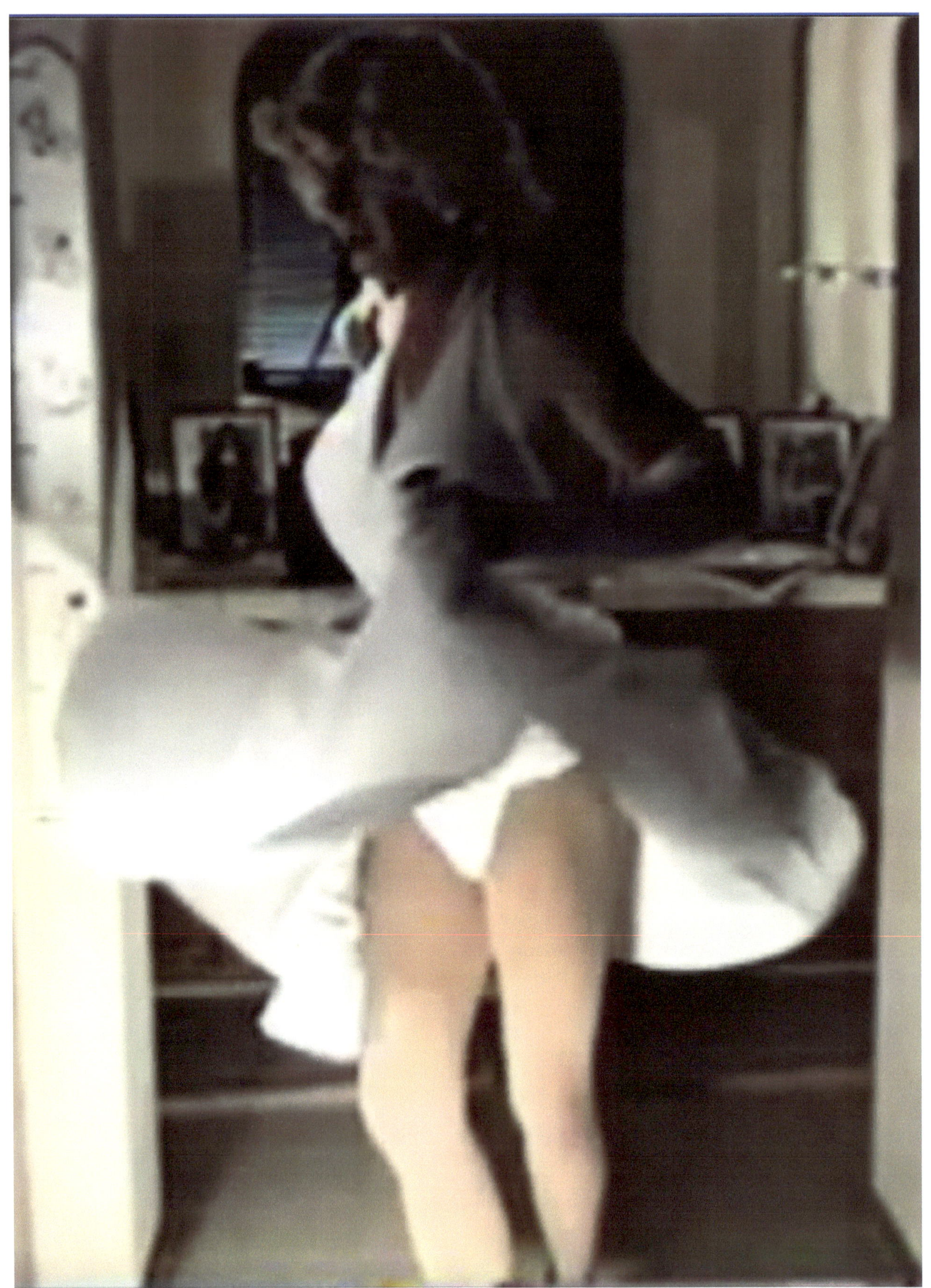

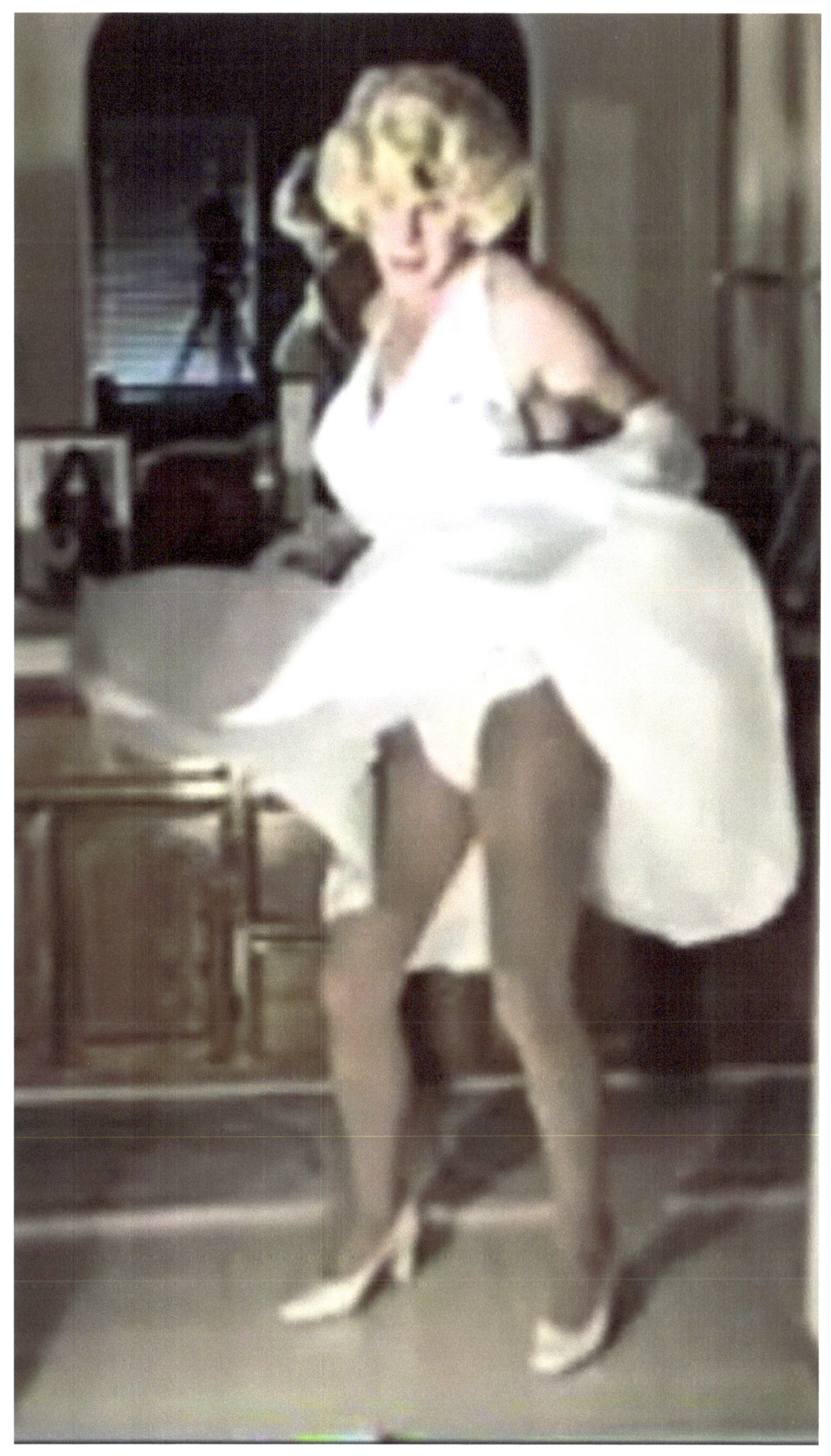

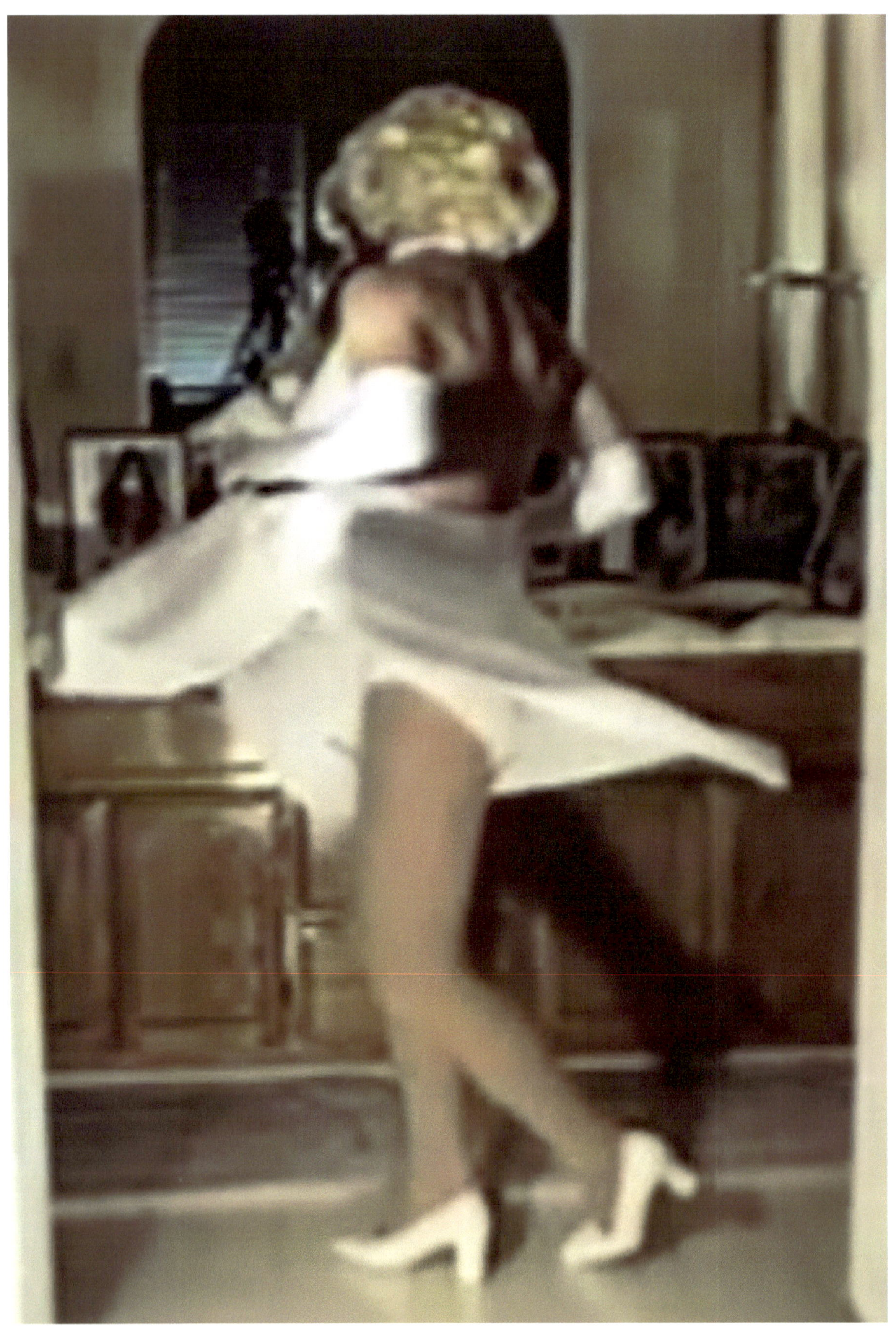

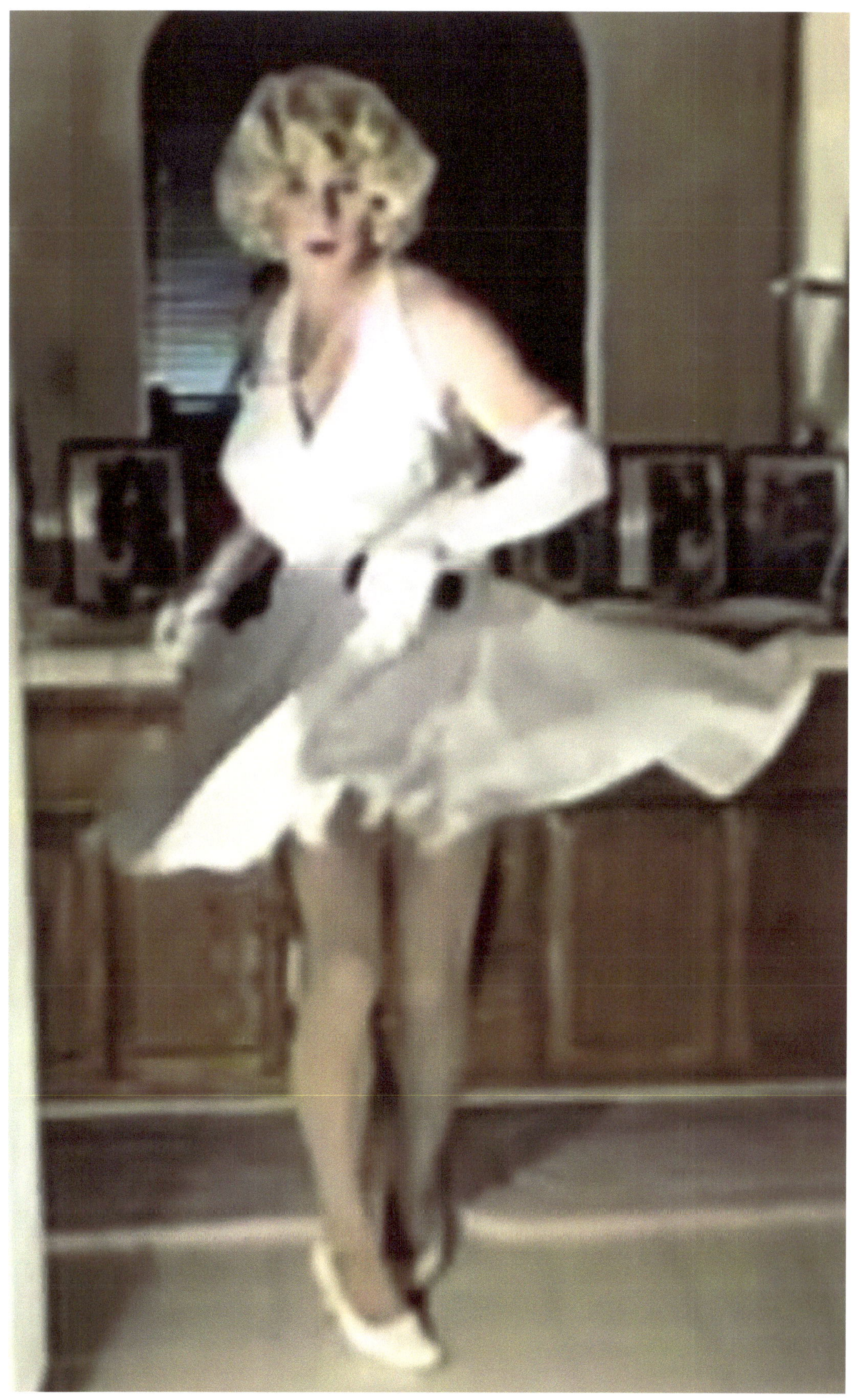

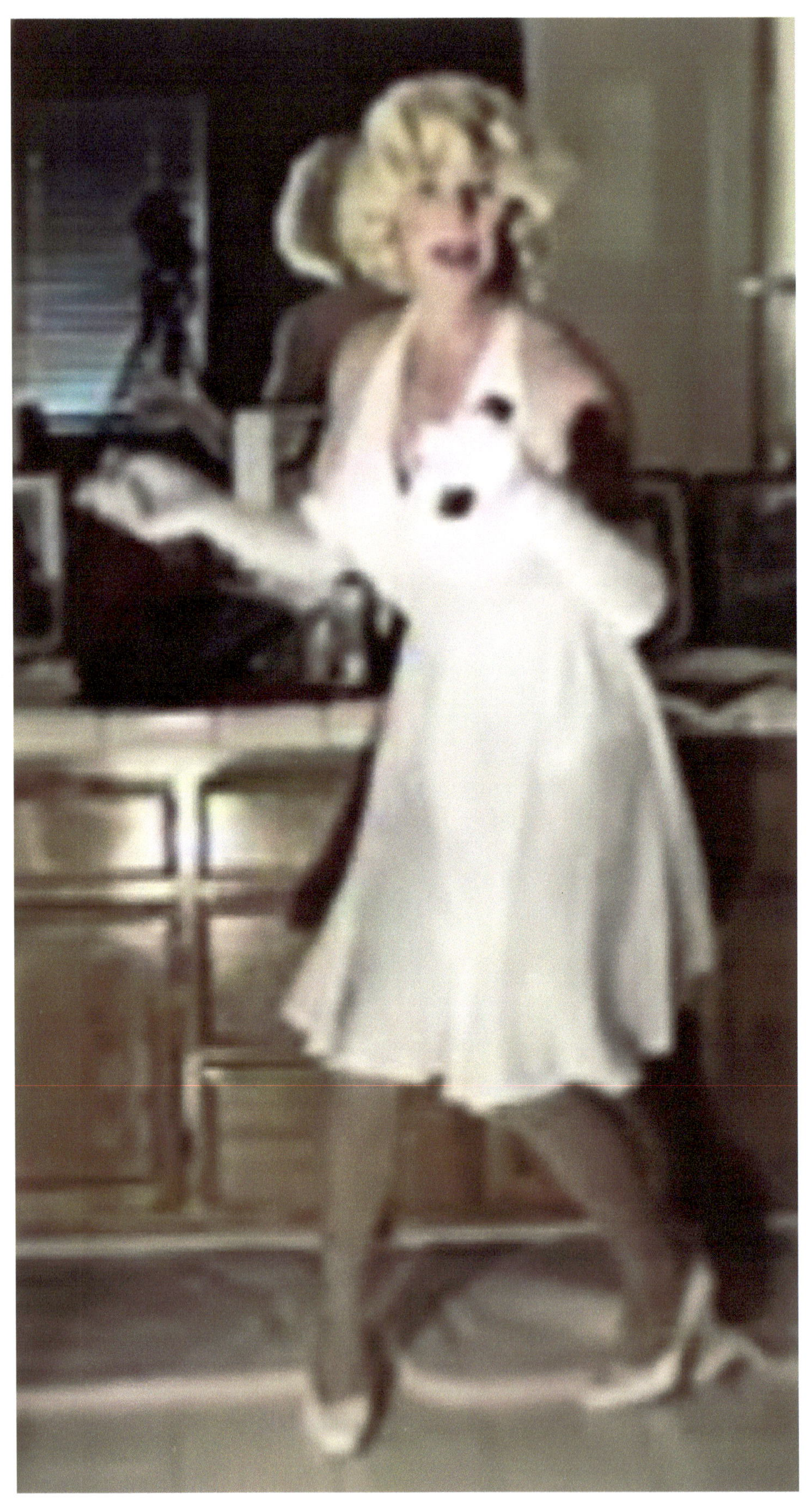

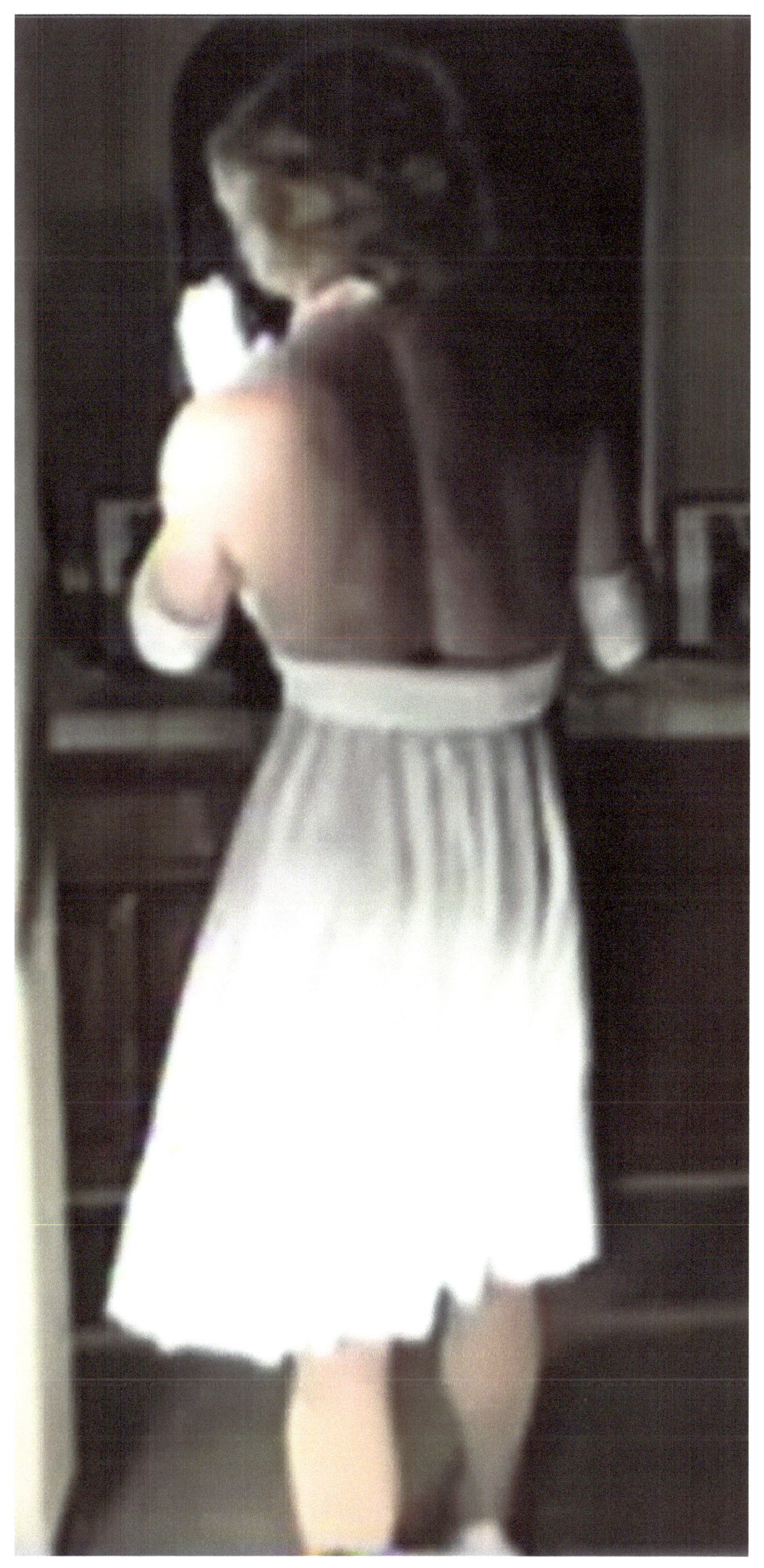

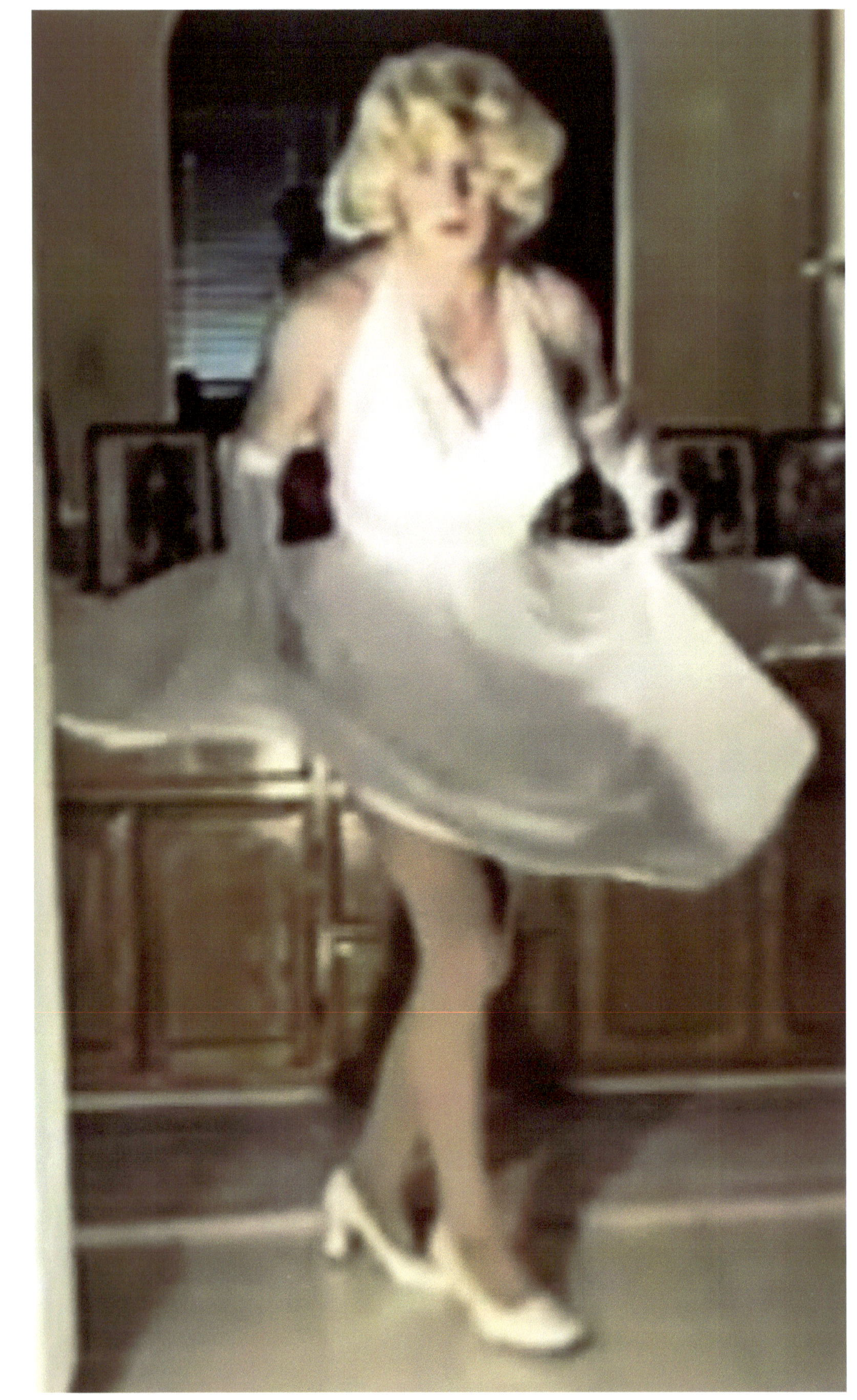

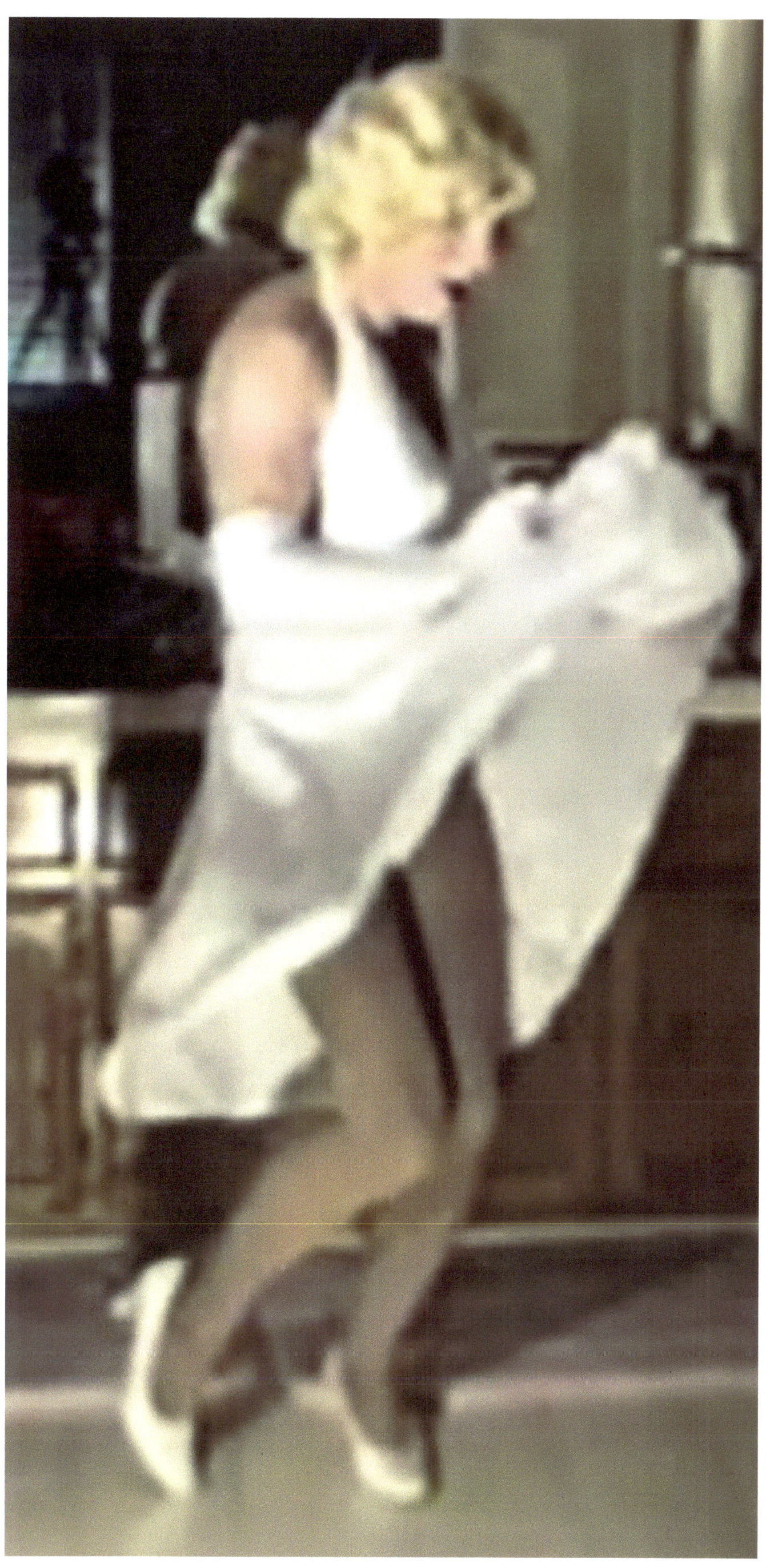

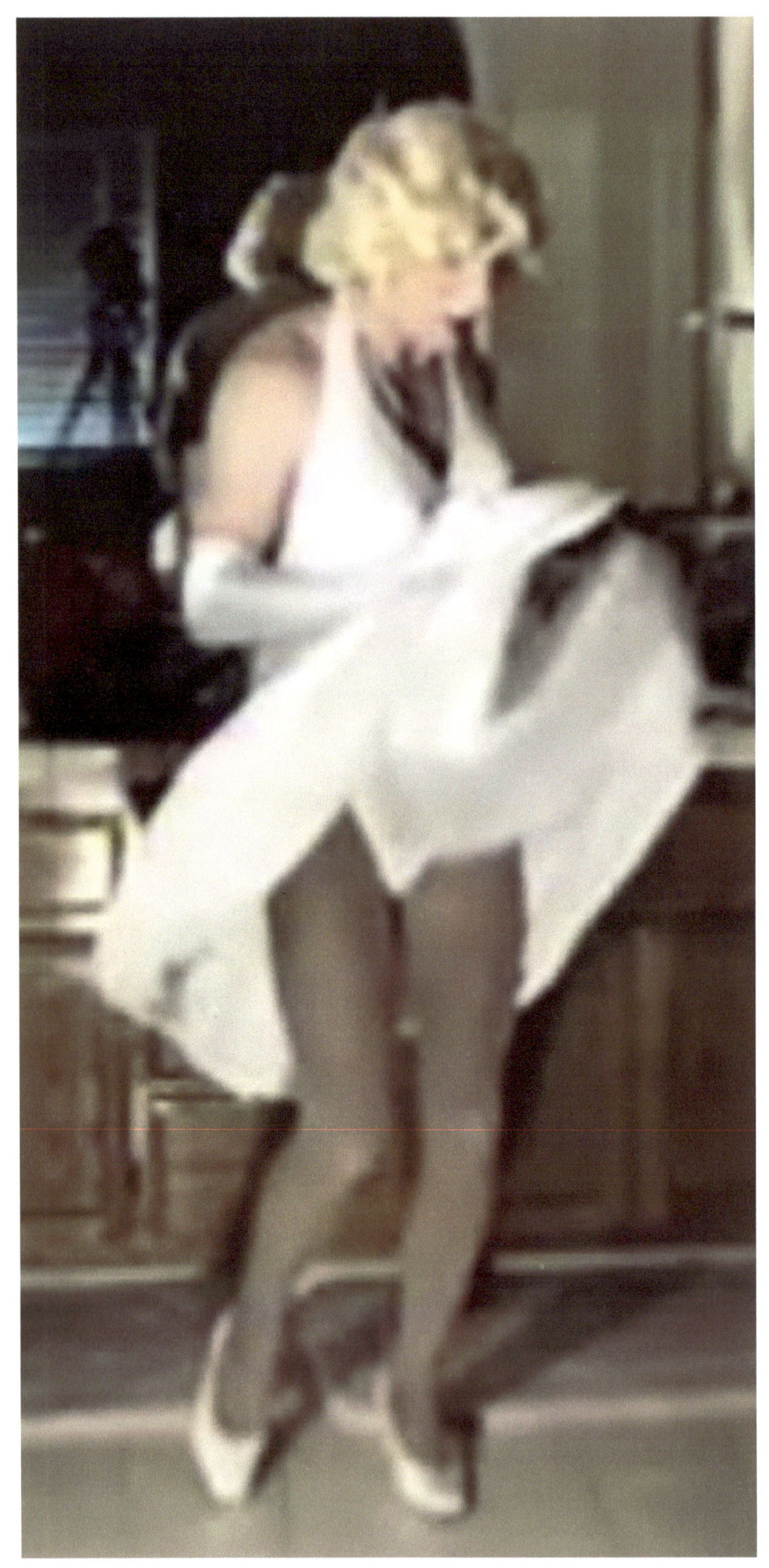

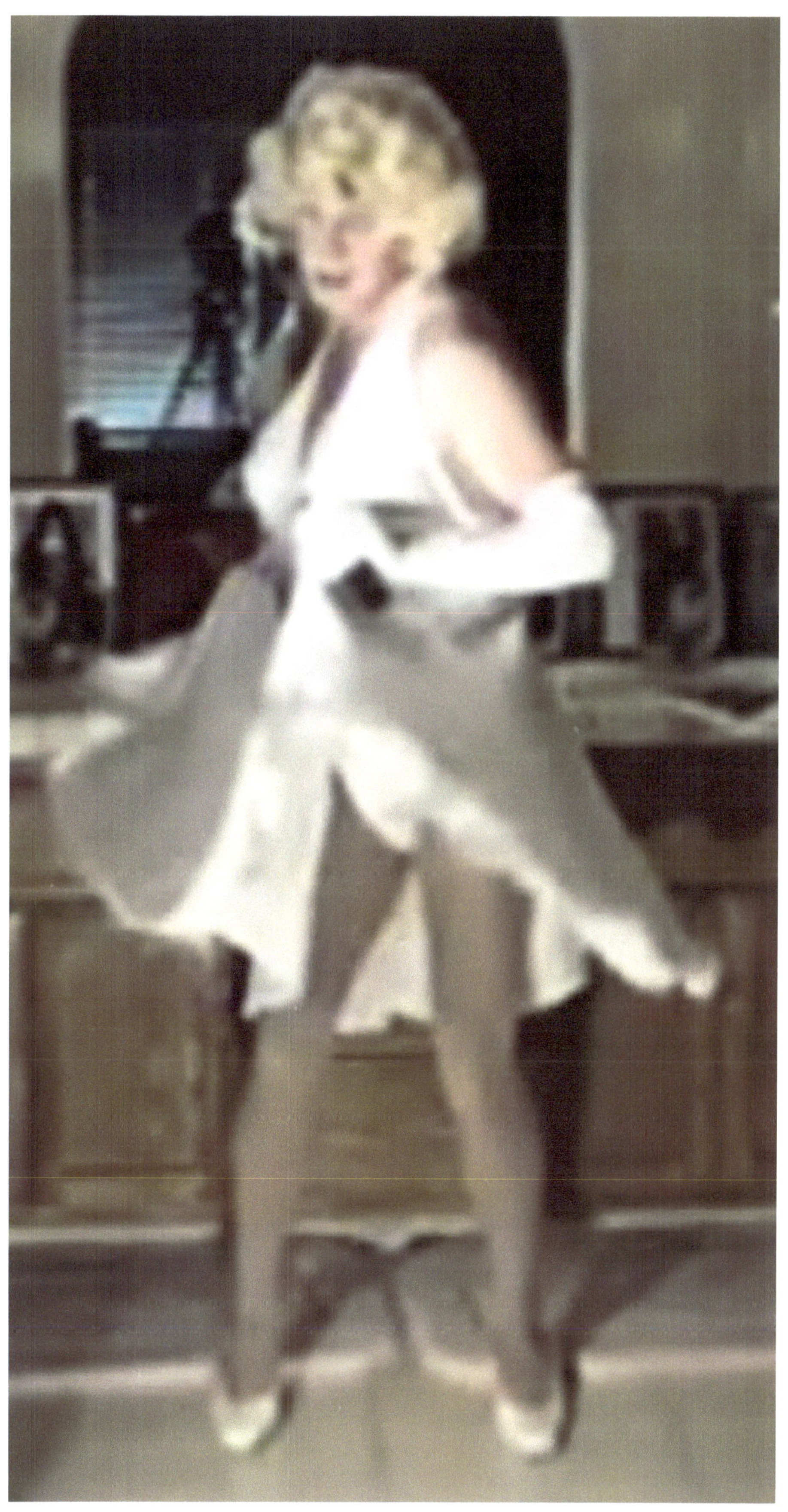

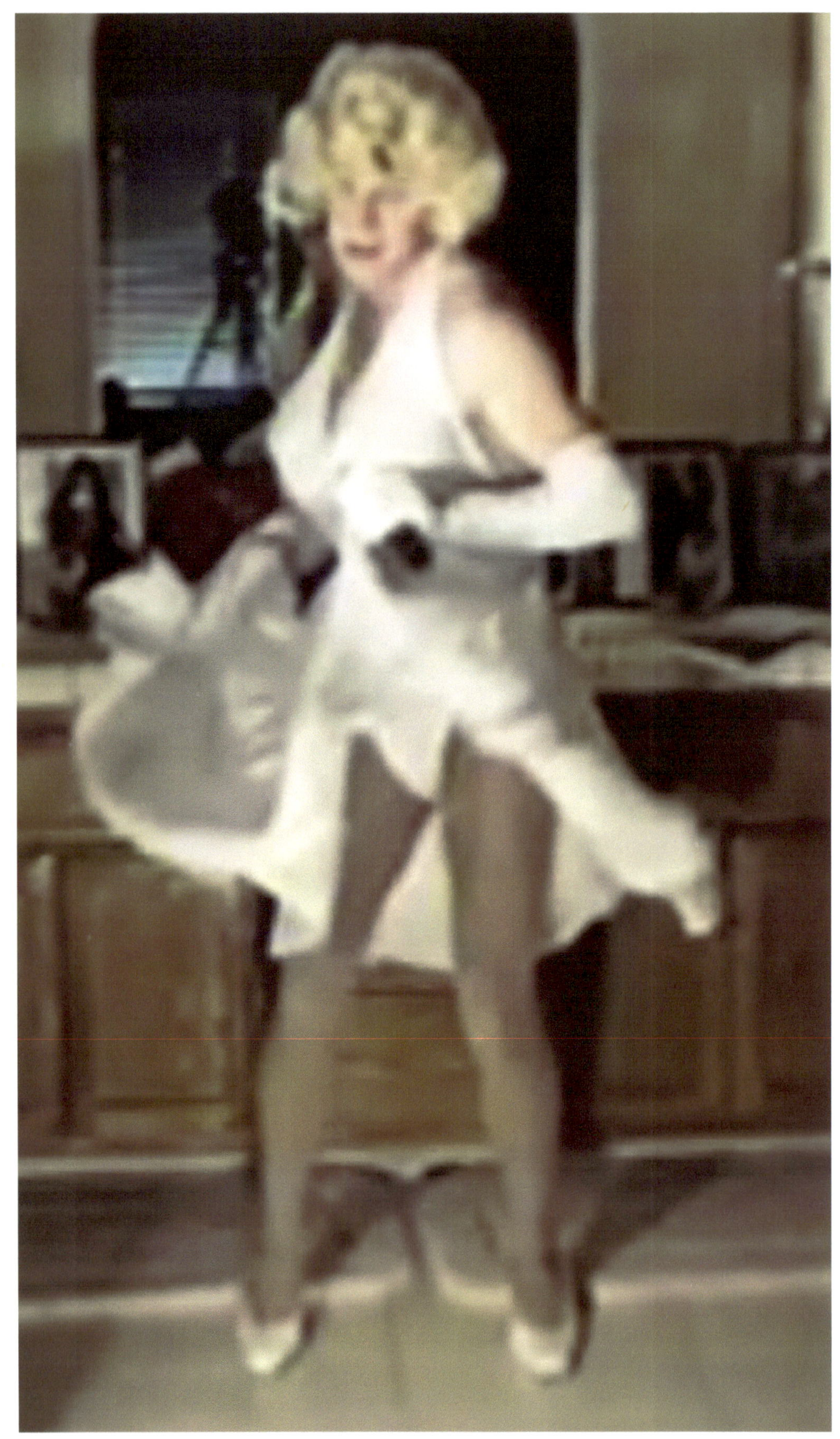

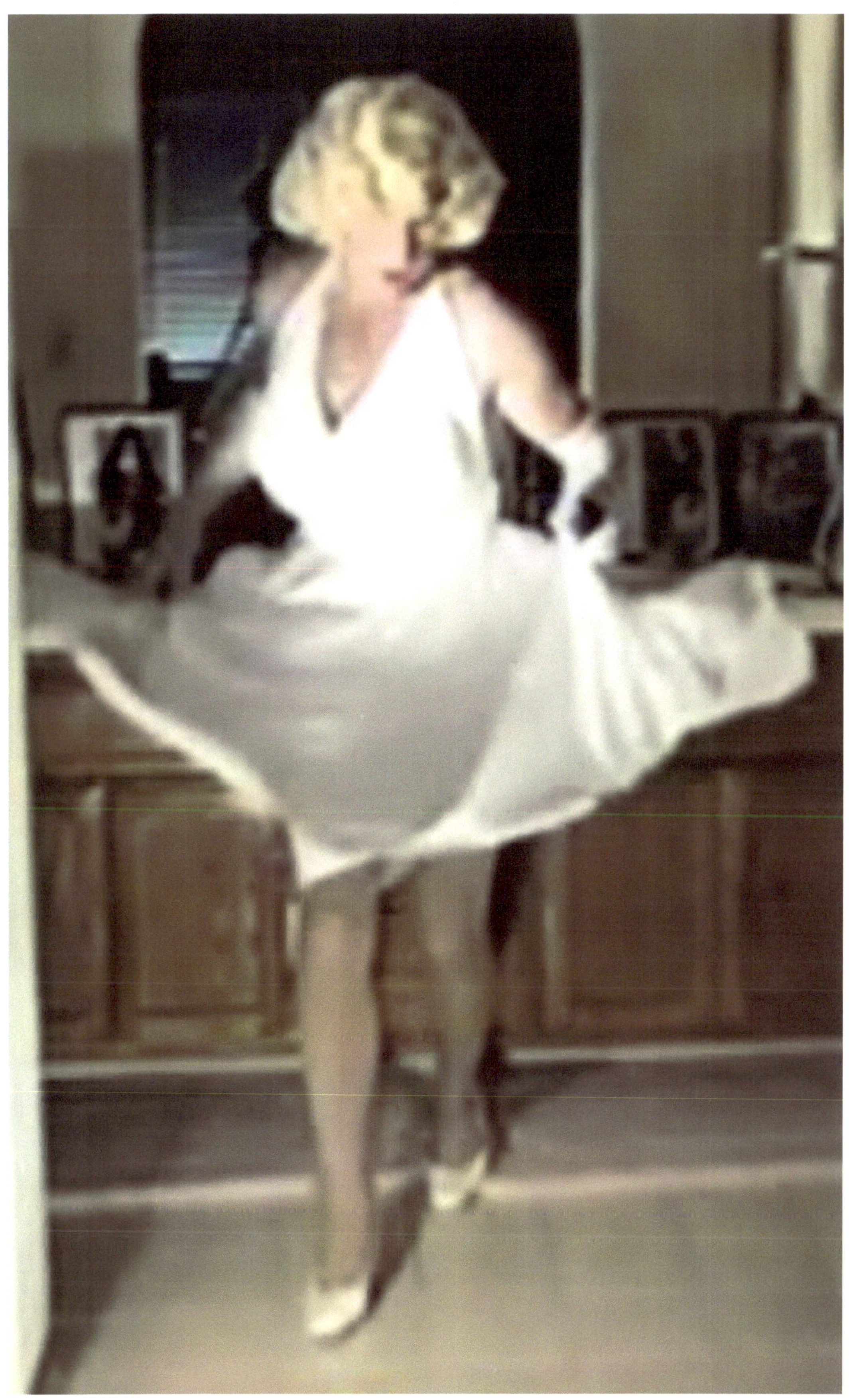

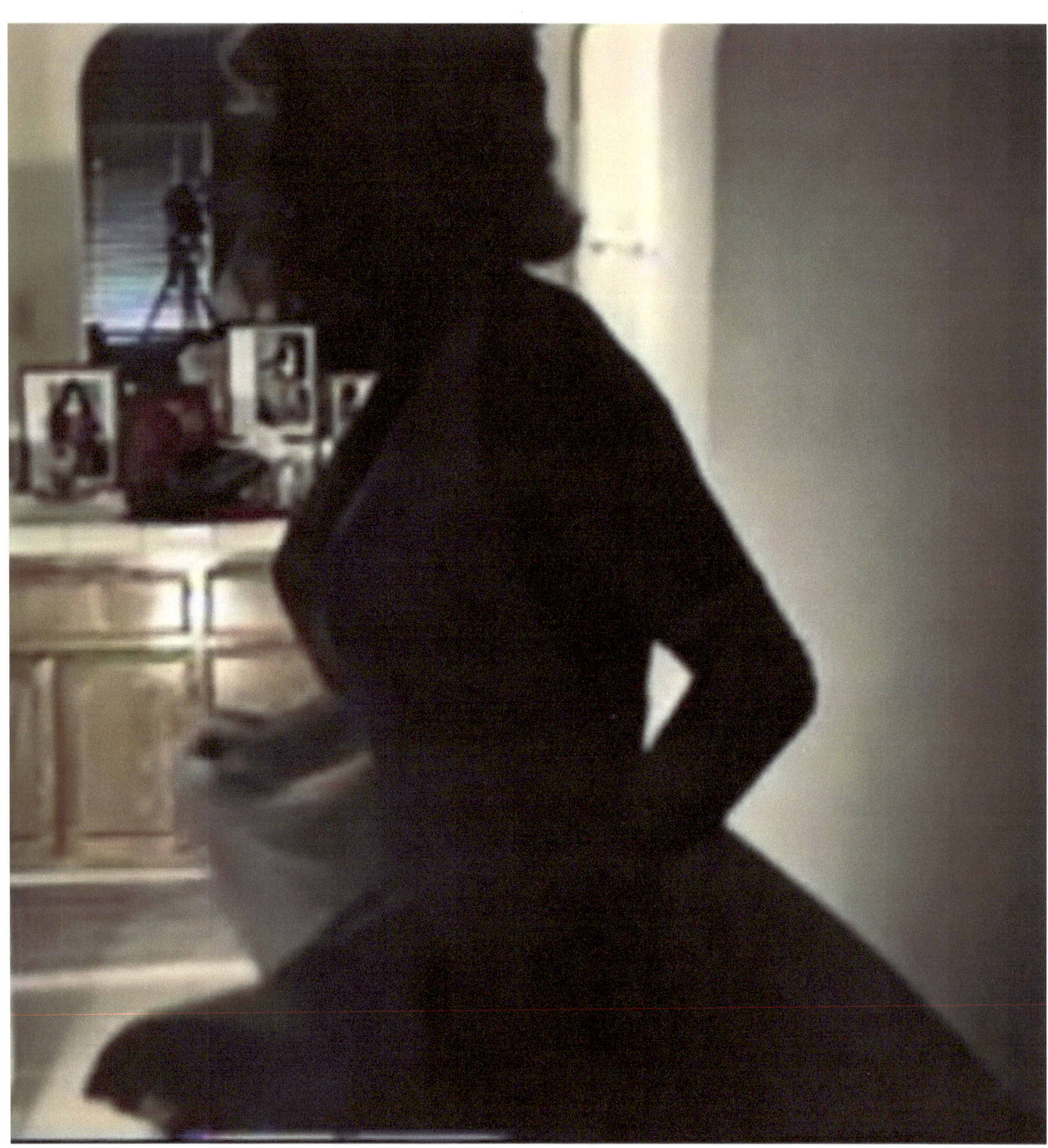

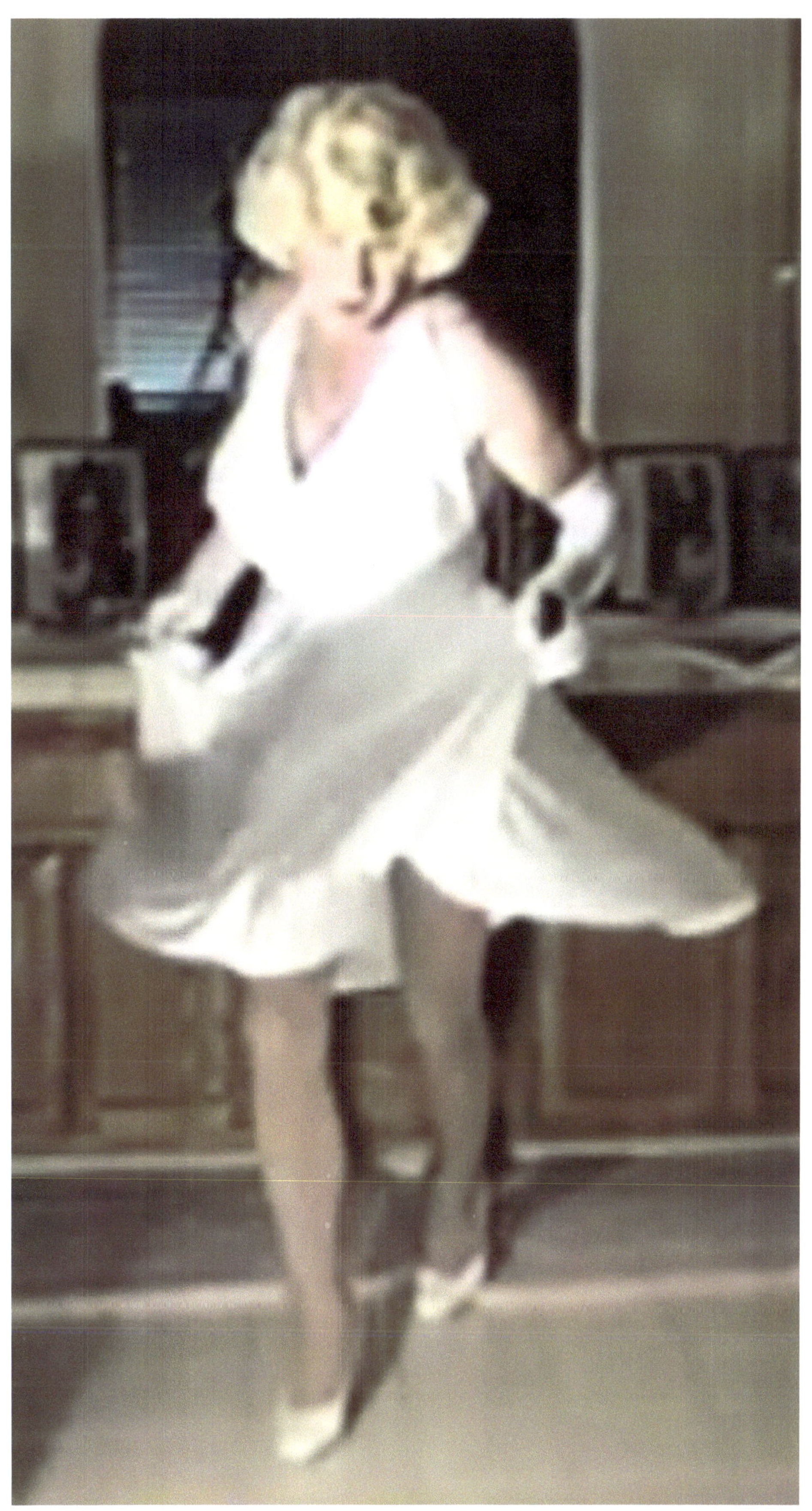

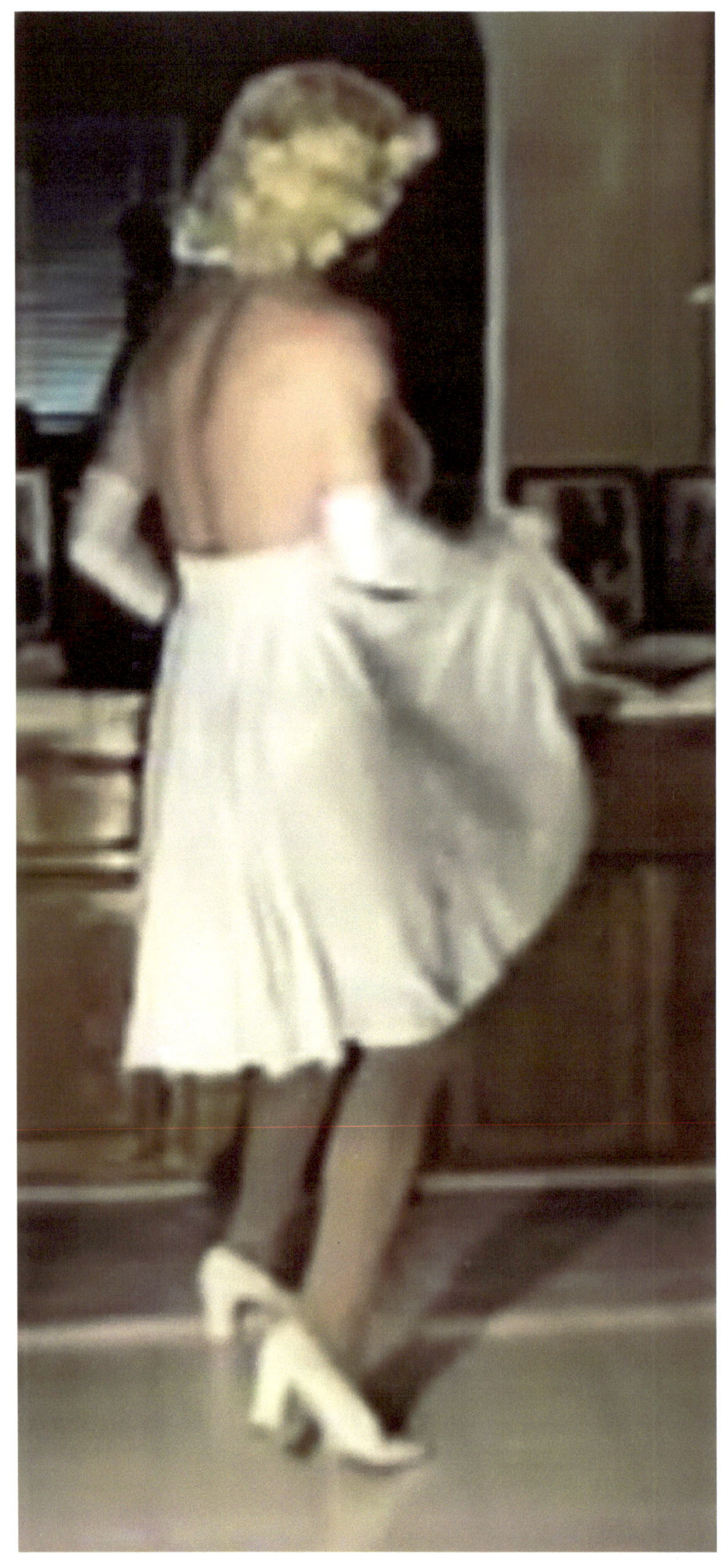

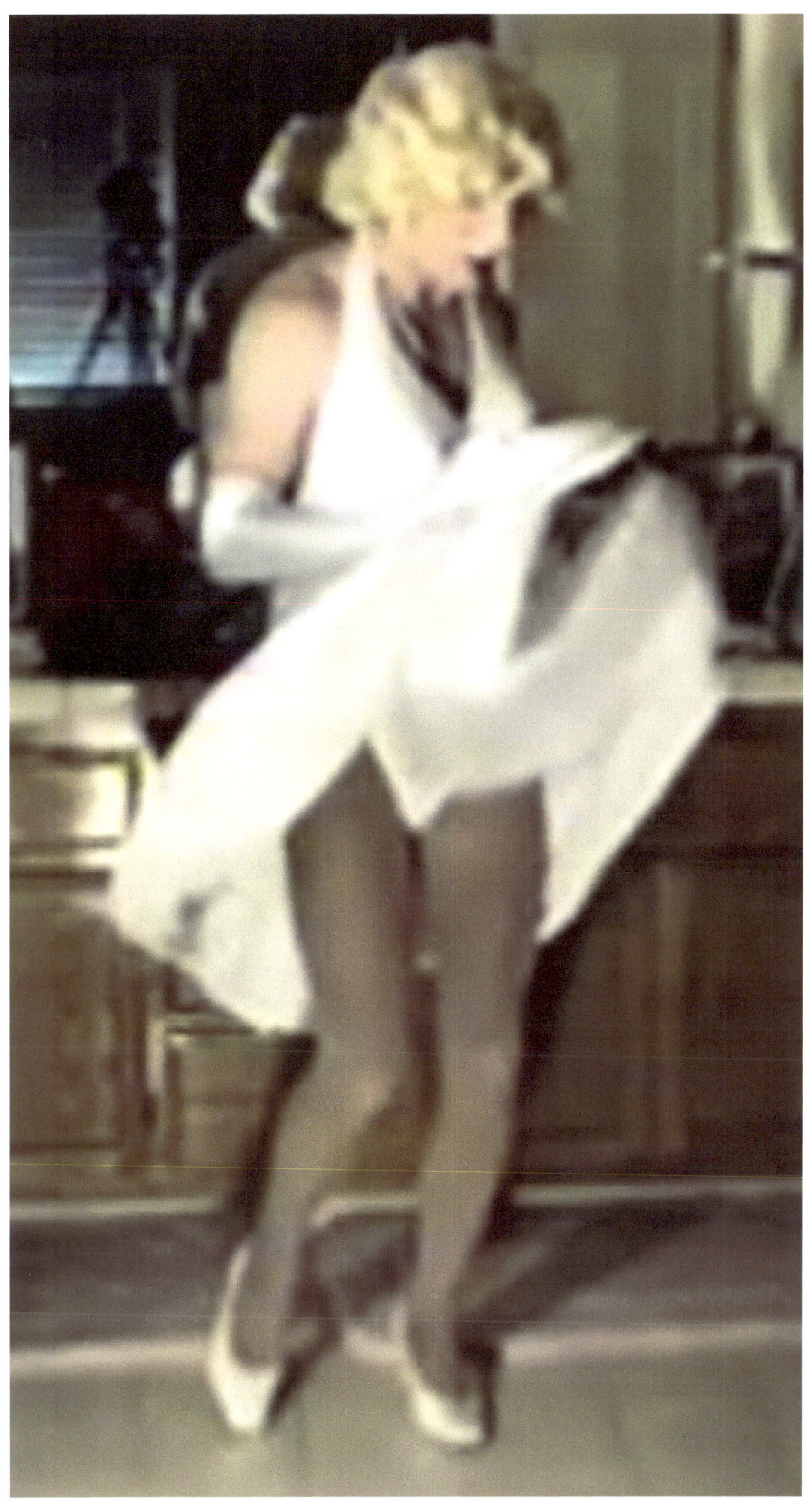

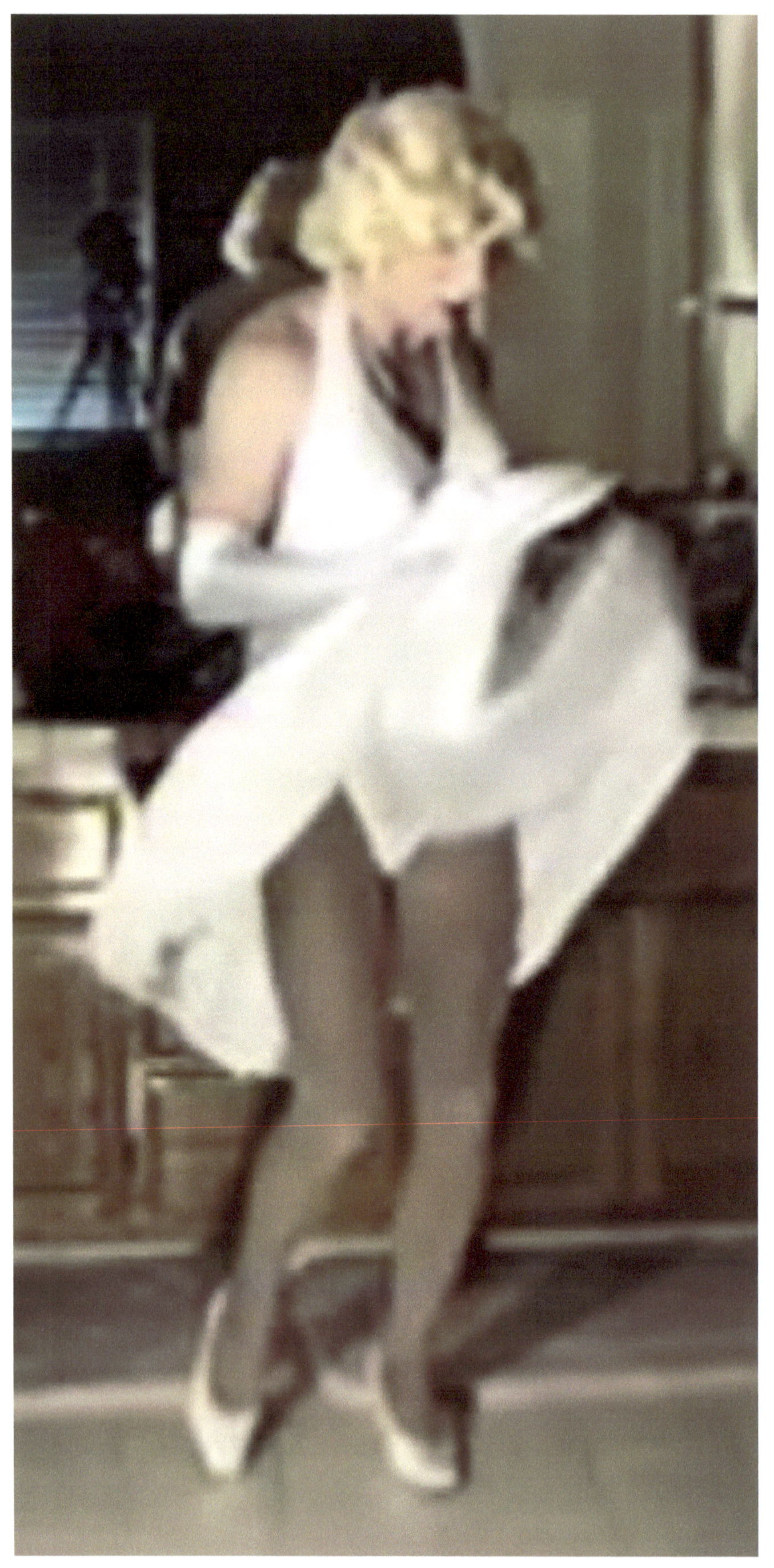

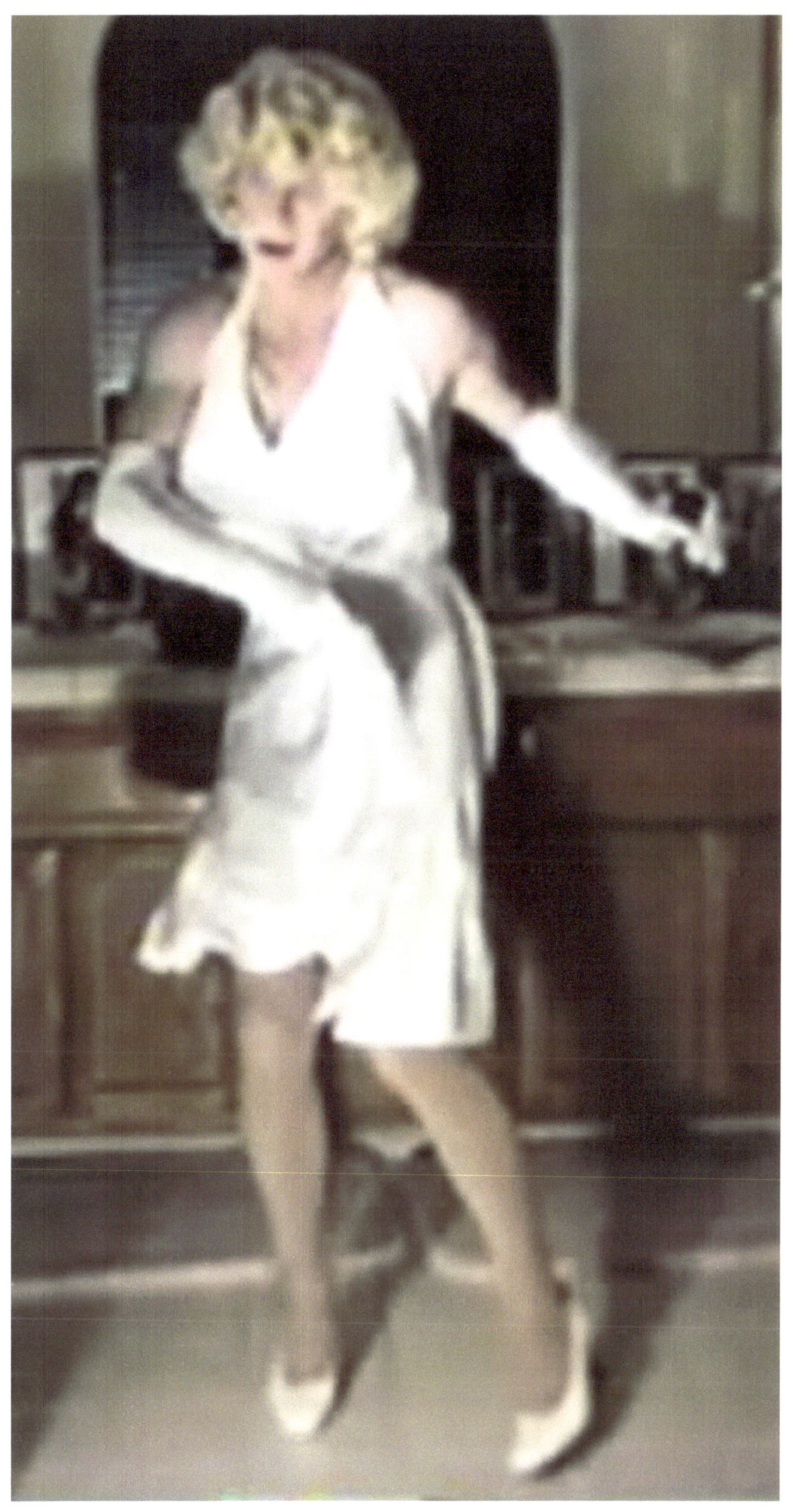

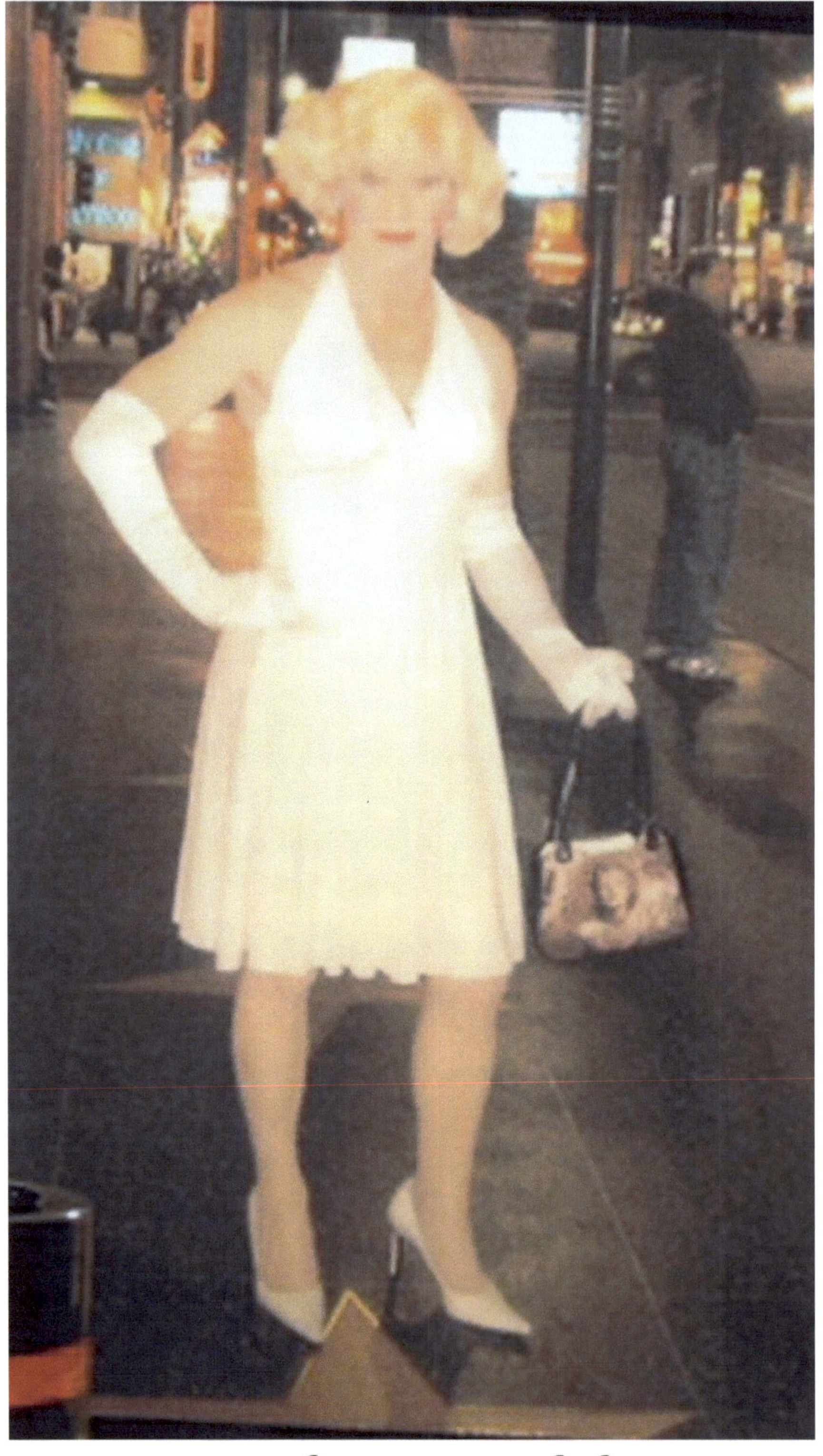

On Hollywood Boulevard I Could Have Been A Star

Transvestite Candy

Candy Stavroulakis